DOVER · THRIFT · EDITIONS

Henry VIII

William Shakespeare

DOVER PUBLICATIONS, INC.
Mineola, New York

DOVER THRIFT EDITIONS

GENERAL EDITOR: MARY CAROLYN WALDREP
EDITOR OF THIS VOLUME: ALISON DAURIO

Bibliographical Note

This Dover edition, first published in 2015, contains the unabridged text of *Henry VIII*, as published in Volume V of *The Macmillan & Co. Edition of the Complete Works of William Shakespeare*, Macmillan & Co., London, 1892. The introductory Note was prepared specially for this edition, and the footnotes from the Macmillan edition have been removed.

International Standard Book Number

ISBN-13: 978-0-486-79692-5
ISBN-10: 0-486-79692-2

Manufactured in the United States by Courier Corporation
79692201   2015
www.doverpublications.com

Note

WILLIAM SHAKESPEARE (1564–1616) was born in Stratford-on-Avon, Warwickshire, England. Although much of his early life remains sketchy, it is known that he moved to London around 1589 to earn his way as an actor and playwright. He joined an acting company known as Lord Chamberlain's Men in 1594, a decision that finally enabled him to share in the financial success of his plays. Only eighteen of his thirty-seven plays were published during his lifetime, and these were usually sold directly to theater companies and printed in quartos, or single-play editions, without his approval.

Written sometime between 1603 and 1613, *Henry VIII* was likely a collaboration between Shakespeare and his contemporary John Fletcher. It imparts the story of the notorious early reign of the ill-famed monarch, and his efforts to secure a divorce from Katharine of Aragon in order to marry Anne Boleyn.

DRAMATIS PERSONÆ

KING HENRY the Eighth.
CARDINAL WOLSEY.
CARDINAL CAMPEIUS.
CAPUCIUS, Ambassador from the Emperor Charles V.
CRANMER, Archbishop of Canterbury.
DUKE OF NORFOLK.
DUKE OF BUCKINGHAM.
DUKE OF SUFFOLK.
EARL OF SURREY.
Lord Chamberlain.
Lord Chancellor.
GARDINER, Bishop of Winchester.
Bishop of Lincoln.
LORD ABERGAVENNY.
LORD SANDS.
SIR HENRY GUILDFORD.
SIR THOMAS LOVELL.
SIR ANTHONY DENNY.
SIR NICHOLAS VAUX.
Secretaries to Wolsey.
CROMWELL, Servant to Wolsey.
GRIFFITH, Gentleman-usher to Queen Katharine.
Three Gentlemen.
DOCTOR BUTTS, Physician to the King.
Garter King-at-Arms.
Surveyor to the Duke of Buckingham.
BRANDON, and a Sergeant-at-Arms.
Door-keeper of the Council-chamber. Porter, and his Man.
Page to Gardiner. A Crier.

QUEEN KATHARINE, wife to King Henry, afterwards divorced.
ANNE BULLEN, her Maid of Honour, afterwards Queen.
An old Lady, friend to Anne Bullen.
PATIENCE, woman to Queen Katharine.

Several Lords and Ladies in the Dumb Shows; Women attending
    upon the Queen; Scribes, Officers, Guards, and other
    Attendants.

Spirits.

SCENE: *London; Westminster; Kimbolton.*

THE PROLOGUE.

I COME no more to make you laugh: things now,
That bear a weighty and a serious brow,
Sad, high and working, full of state and woe,
Such noble scenes as draw the eye to flow,
We now present. Those that can pity, here
May, if they think it well, let fall a tear;
The subject will deserve it. Such as give
Their money out of hope they may believe,
May here find truth too. Those that come to see
Only a show or two, and so agree   10
The play may pass, if they be still and willing,
I'll undertake may see away their shilling
Richly in two short hours. Only they
That come to hear a merry bawdy play,
A noise of targets, or to see a fellow
In a long motley coat guarded with yellow,
Will be deceived; for, gentle hearers, know,
To rank our chosen truth with such a show
As fool and fight is, beside forfeiting
Our own brains and the opinion that we bring   20
To make that only true we now intend,
Will leave us never an understanding friend.
Therefore, for goodness' sake, and as you are known
The first and happiest hearers of the town,
Be sad, as we would make ye: think ye see
The very persons of our noble story
As they were living; think you see them great,
And follow'd with the general throng and sweat

Of thousand friends; then, in a moment, see
How soon this mightiness meets misery: 30
And if you can be merry then, I'll say
A man may weep upon his wedding-day.

ACT I.

Scene I. *London. An Ante-Chamber in the Palace.*

Enter the DUKE OF NORFOLK *at one door; at the other, the* DUKE OF BUCKINGHAM *and the* LORD ABERGAVENNY.

BUCK. Good morrow, and well met. How have ye done
Since last we saw in France?

NOR.   I thank your grace,
Healthful, and ever since a fresh admirer
Of what I saw there.

BUCK.   An untimely ague
Stay'd me a prisoner in my chamber, when
Those suns of glory, those two lights of men,
Met in the vale of Andren.

NOR.   'Twixt Guynes and Arde:
I was then present, saw them salute on horseback;
Beheld them, when they 'lighted, how they clung
In their embracement, as they grew together;   10
Which had they, what four throned ones could have weigh'd
Such a compounded one?

BUCK.   All the whole time
I was my chamber's prisoner.

NOR.   Then you lost
The view of earthly glory: men might say,
Till this time pomp was single, but now married
To one above itself. Each following day
Became the next day's master, till the last
Made former wonders its. To-day the French,
All clinquant, all in gold, like heathen gods,
Shone down the English; and to-morrow they   20
Made Britain India: every man that stood
Show'd like a mine. Their dwarfish pages were
As cherubins, all gilt: the madams too,
Not used to toil, did almost sweat to bear
The pride upon them, that their very labour
Was to them as a painting: now this masque
Was cried incomparable; and the ensuing night
Made it a fool and beggar. The two kings,

3

Equal in lustre, were now best, now worst,
As presence did present them; him in eye　　　　　　　　30
Still him in praise; and being present both,
'Twas said they saw but one, and no discerner
Durst wag his tongue in censure. When these suns—
For so they phrase 'em—by their heralds challenged
The noble spirits to arms, they did perform
Beyond thought's compass; that former fabulous story,
Being now seen possible enough, got credit,
That Bevis was believed.
　　　BUCK.　　　　　　　　　O, you go far.
　　　NOR. As I belong to worship, and affect
In honour honesty, the tract of every thing　　　　　　40
Would by a good discourser lose some life,
Which action's self was tongue to. All was royal;
To the disposing of it nought rebell'd;
Order gave each thing view; the office did
Distinctly his full function.
　　　BUCK.　　　　　　　　　Who did guide,
I mean, who set the body and the limbs
Of this great sport together, as you guess?
　　　NOR. One, certes, that promises no element
In such a business.
　　　BUCK.　　　　　　I pray you, who, my lord?
　　　NOR. All this was order'd by the good discretion　　50
Of the right reverend Cardinal of York.
　　　BUCK. The devil speed him! no man's pie is freed
From his ambitious finger. What had he
To do in these fierce vanities? I wonder
That such a keech can with his very bulk
Take up the rays o' the beneficial sun,
And keep it from the earth.
　　　NOR.　　　　　　　　　Surely, sir,
There's in him stuff that puts him to these ends;
For, being not propp'd by ancestry, whose grace
Chalks successors their way, nor call'd upon　　　　　60
For high feats done to the crown; neither allied
To eminent assistants; but, spider-like,
Out of his self-drawing web, he gives us note,
The force of his own merit makes his way;
A gift that heaven gives for him, which buys

A place next to the king.

ABER.   I cannot tell
What heaven hath given him; let some graver eye
Pierce into that; but I can see his pride
Peep through each part of him: whence has he that?
If not from hell, the devil is a niggard,   70
Or has given all before, and he begins
A new hell in himself.

BUCK.   Why the devil,
Upon this French going out, took he upon him,
Without the privity o' the king, to appoint
Who should attend on him? He makes up the file
Of all the gentry; for the most part such
To whom as great a charge as little honour
He meant to lay upon: and his own letter,
The honourable board of council out,
Must fetch him in he papers.

ABER.   I do know   80
Kinsmen of mine, three at the least, that have
By this so sicken'd their estates that never
They shall abound as formerly.

BUCK.   O, many
Have broke their backs with laying manors on 'em
For this great journey. What did this vanity
But minister communication of
A most poor issue?

NOR.   Grievingly I think,
The peace between the French and us not values
The cost that did conclude it.

BUCK.   Every man,
After the hideous storm that follow'd, was   90
A thing inspired, and not consulting broke
Into a general prophecy: That this tempest,
Dashing the garment of this peace, aboded
The sudden breach on 't.

NOR.   Which is budded out;
For France hath flaw'd the league, and hath attach'd
Our merchants' goods at Bourdeaux.

ABER.   Is it therefore
The ambassador is silenced?

NOR.   Marry, is 't.

ABER. A proper title of a peace, and purchased
At a superfluous rate!

BUCK.   Why, all this business
Our reverend cardinal carried.

NOR.   Like it your grace,   100
The state takes notice of the private difference
Betwixt you and the cardinal. I advise you—
And take it from a heart that wishes towards you
Honour and plenteous safety—that you read
The cardinal's malice and his potency
Together; to consider further that
What his high hatred would effect wants not
A minister in his power. You know his nature,
That he's revengeful, and I know his sword
Hath a sharp edge; it's long and 't may be said   110
It reaches far, and where 'twill not extend,
Thither he darts it. Bosom up my counsel;
You 'll find it wholesome. Lo, where comes that rock
That I advise your shunning.

Enter CARDINAL WOLSEY, *the purse borne before him, certain of the*
    Guard, *and two* Secretaries *with papers. The* CARDINAL *in his*
    passage fixeth his eye on BUCKINGHAM, *and* BUCKINGHAM *on*
    him, both full of disdain.

WOL. The Duke of Buckingham's surveyor, ha?
Where 's his examination?

FIRST SEC.   Here, so please you.

WOL. Is he in person ready?

FIRST SEC.   Ay, please your grace.

WOL. Well, we shall then know more; and Buckingham
Shall lessen this big look.   [*Exeunt Wolsey and his Train.*

BUCK. This butcher's cur is venom-mouth'd, and I   120
Have not the power to muzzle him; therefore best
Not wake him in his slumber. A beggar's book
Outworths a noble's blood.

NOR.   What, are you chafed?
Ask God for temperance; that's the appliance only
Which your disease requires.

BUCK.   I read in 's looks

Matter against me, and his eye reviled
Me as his abject object: at this instant
He bores me with some trick: he's gone to the king;
I'll follow and outstare him.

NOR.   Stay, my lord,
And let your reason with your choler question   130
What 'tis you go about: to climb steep hills
Requires slow pace at first: anger is like
A full-hot horse, who being allow'd his way,
Self-mettle tires him. Not a man in England
Can advise me like you: be to yourself
As you would to your friend.

BUCK.   I'll to the king;
And from a mouth of honour quite cry down
This Ipswich fellow's insolence, or proclaim
There's difference in no persons.

NOR.   Be advised;
Heat not a furnace for your foe so hot   140
That it do singe yourself: we may outrun,
By violent swiftness, that which we run at,
And lose by over-running. Know you not,
The fire that mounts the liquor till 't run o'er
In seeming to augment it wastes it? Be advised:
I say again, there is no English soul
More stronger to direct you than yourself,
If with the sap of reason you would quench,
Or but allay, the fire of passion.

BUCK.   Sir,
I am thankful to you; and I'll go along   150
By your prescription: but this top-proud fellow—
Whom from the flow of gall I name not, but
From sincere motions—by intelligence
And proofs as clear as founts in July when
We see each grain of gravel, I do know
To be corrupt and treasonous.

NOR.   Say not 'treasonous.'

BUCK. To the king I 'll say 't; and make my vouch as strong
As shore of rock. Attend. This holy fox,
Or wolf, or both—for he is equal ravenous
As he is subtle, and as prone to mischief   160

As able to perform 't; his mind and place
Infecting one another, yea, reciprocally—
Only to show his pomp as well in France
As here at home, suggests the king our master
To this last costly treaty, the interview,
That swallow'd so much treasure, and like a glass
Did break i' the rinsing.

NOR.   Faith, and so it did.

 BUCK. Pray, give me favour, sir. This cunning cardinal
The articles o' the combination drew
As himself pleased; and they were ratified   170
As he cried 'Thus let be,' to as much end
As give a crutch to the dead: but our count-cardinal
Has done this, and 'tis well; for worthy Wolsey,
Who cannot err, he did it. Now this follows—
Which, as I take it, is a kind of puppy
To the old dam, treason—Charles the emperor,
Under pretence to see the queen his aunt—
For 'twas indeed his colour, but he came
To whisper Wolsey—here makes visitation:
His fears were that the interview betwixt   180
England and France might through their amity
Breed him some prejudice; for from this league
Peep'd harms that menaced him: he privily
Deals with our cardinal; and, as I trow—
Which I do well, for I am sure the emperor
Paid ere he promised; whereby his suit was granted
Ere it was ask'd—but when the way was made
And paved with gold, the emperor thus desired,
That he would please to alter the king's course,
And break the foresaid peace. Let the king know,   190
As soon he shall by me, that thus the cardinal
Does buy and sell his honour as he pleases,
And for his own advantage.

 NOR.   I am sorry
To hear this of him, and could wish he were
Something mistaken in 't.

 BUCK.   No, not a syllable:
I do pronounce him in that very shape
He shall appear in proof.

Enter BRANDON, *a* Sergeant at arms *before him, and two or three of the* Guard.

BRAN. Your office, sergeant; execute it.
SERG.   Sir,
My lord the Duke of Buckingham, and Earl
Of Hereford, Stafford, and Northampton, I   200
Arrest thee of high treason, in the name
Of our most sovereign king.
BUCK.   Lo you, my lord,
The net has fall'n upon me! I shall perish
Under device and practice.
BRAN.   I am sorry
To see you ta'en from liberty, to look on
The business present: 'tis his highness' pleasure
You shall to the Tower.
BUCK.   It will help me nothing
To plead mine innocence; for that dye is on me
Which makes my whitest part black. The will of heaven
Be done in this and all things! I obey.   210
O my Lord Abergavenny, fare you well!
BRAN. Nay, he must bear you company. [*To Abergavenny*] The king
Is pleased you shall to the Tower, till you know
How he determines further.
ABER.   As the duke said,
The will of heaven be done, and the king's pleasure
By me obey'd!
BRAN.   Here is a warrant from
The king to attach Lord Montacute; and the bodies
Of the duke's confessor, John de la Car,
One Gilbert Peck, his chancellor,—
BUCK.   So, so;
These are the limbs o' the plot: no more, I hope.   220
BRAN. A monk o' the Chartreux.
BUCK.   O, Nicholas Hopkins?
BRAN.   He.
BUCK. My surveyor is false; the o'er-great cardinal
Hath show'd him gold; my life is spann'd already:
I am the shadow of poor Buckingham,

Whose figure even this instant cloud puts on,
By darkening my clear sun. My lord, farewell. [*Exeunt.*

SCENE II. *The Same. The Council-Chamber.*

Cornets. Enter KING HENRY, *leaning on the* CARDINAL'S *shoulder;
the Nobles, and* SIR THOMAS LOVELL: *the* CARDINAL *places
himself under the* KING'S *feet on his right side.*

KING. My life itself, and the best heart of it,
Thanks you for this great care: I stood i' the level
Of a full-charged confederacy, and give thanks
To you that choked it. Let be call'd before us
That gentleman of Buckingham's; in person
I 'll hear him his confessions justify;
And point by point the treasons of his master
He shall again relate.

A noise within, crying 'Room for the Queen!' *Enter* QUEEN
KATHARINE, *ushered by the* DUKE OF NORFOLK, *and the* DUKE
OF SUFFOLK: *she kneels. The* KING *riseth from his state, takes her
up, kisses and placeth her by him.*

Q. KATH. Nay, we must longer kneel: I am a suitor.
KING. Arise, and take place by us: half your suit   10
Never name to us; you have half our power:
The other moiety ere you ask is given;
Repeat your will and take it.
Q. KATH.   Thank your majesty.
That you would love yourself, and in that love
Not unconsider'd leave your honour nor
The dignity of your office, is the point
Of my petition.
KING.   Lady mine, proceed.
Q. KATH. I am solicited, not by a few,
And those of true condition, that your subjects
Are in great grievance: there have been commissions   20

Sent down among 'em, which hath flaw'd the heart
Of all their loyalties: wherein although,
My good lord cardinal, they vent reproaches
Most bitterly on you as putter on
Of these exactions, yet the king our master—
Whose honour heaven shield from soil!—even he escapes not
Language unmannerly, yea, such which breaks
The sides of loyalty, and almost appears
In loud rebellion.

    Nor.   Not almost appears;
It doth appear; for, upon these taxations,   30
The clothiers all, not able to maintain
The many to them 'longing, have put off
The spinsters, carders, fullers, weavers, who,
Unfit for other life, compell'd by hunger
And lack of other means, in desperate manner
Daring the event to the teeth, are all in uproar,
And danger serves among them.

    King.   Taxation!
Wherein? and what taxation? My lord cardinal,
You that are blamed for it alike with us,
Know you of this taxation?

    Wol.   Please you, sir,   40
I know but of a single part in aught
Pertains to the state, and front but in that file
Where others tell steps with me.

    Q. Kath.   No, my lord,
You know no more than others: but you frame
Things that are known alike, which are not wholesome
To those which would not know them, and yet must
Perforce be their acquaintance. These exactions,
Whereof my sovereign would have note, they are
Most pestilent to the hearing; and, to bear 'em,
The back is sacrifice to the load. They say   50
They are devised by you; or else you suffer
Too hard an exclamation.

    King.   Still exaction!
The nature of it? in what kind, let 's know,
Is this exaction?

    Q. Kath.   I am much too venturous

In tempting of your patience, but am bolden'd
Under your promised pardon. The subjects' grief
Comes through commissions, which compel from each
The sixth part of his substance, to be levied
Without delay; and the pretence for this
Is named your wars in France: this makes bold mouths: 60
Tongues spit their duties out, and cold hearts freeze
Allegiance in them; their curses now
Live where their prayers did; and it 's come to pass,
This tractable obedience is a slave
To each incensed will. I would your highness
Would give it quick consideration, for
There is no primer business.
    KING.   By my life,
This is against our pleasure.
    WOL.   And for me,
I have no further gone in this than by
A single voice, and that not pass'd me but   70
By learned approbation of the judges. If I am
Traduced by ignorant tongues, which neither know
My faculties nor person, yet will be
The chronicles of my doing, let me say
'Tis but the fate of place, and the rough brake
That virtue must go through. We must not stint
Our necessary actions, in the fear
To cope malicious censurers; which ever,
As ravenous fishes, do a vessel follow
That is new-trimm'd, but benefit no further   80
Than vainly longing. What we oft do best,
By sick interpreters, once weak ones, is
Not ours or not allow'd; what worst, as oft,
Hitting a grosser quality, is cried up
For our best act. If we shall stand still,
In fear our notion will be mock'd or carp'd at,
We should take root here where we sit, or sit
State-statues only.
    KING.   Things done well,
And with a care, exempt themselves from fear;
Things done without example, in their issue   90
Are to be fear'd. Have you a precedent
Of this commission? I believe, not any.

We must not rend our subjects from our laws,
And stick them in our will. Sixth part of each?
A trembling contribution! Why, we take
From every tree lop, bark, and part o' the timber,
And though we leave it with a root, thus hack'd,
The air will drink the sap. To every county
Where this is question'd send our letters, with
Free pardon to each man that has denied   100
The force of this commission: pray, look to 't;
I put it to your care.
  WOL.   [*To the Secretary*] A word with you.
Let there be letters writ to every shire,
Of the king's grace and pardon. The grieved commons
Hardly conceive of me: let it be noised
That through our intercession this revokement
And pardon comes: I shall anon advise you
Further in the proceeding.   [*Exit Secretary*.

Enter Surveyor.

  Q. KATH. I am sorry that the Duke of Buckingham
Is run in your displeasure.
  KING.   It grieves many: 110
The gentleman is learn'd and a most rare speaker;
To nature none more bound; his training such
That he may furnish and instruct great teachers,
And never seek for aid out of himself. Yet see,
When these so noble benefits shall prove
Not well disposed, the mind growing once corrupt,
They turn to vicious forms, ten times more ugly
Than ever they were fair. This man so complete,
Who was enroll'd 'mongst wonders, and when we,
Almost with ravish'd listening, could not find   120
His hour of speech a minute; he, my lady,
Hath into monstrous habits put the graces
That once were his, and is become as black
As if besmear'd in hell. Sit by us; you shall hear—
This was his gentleman in trust—of him
Things to strike honour sad. Bid him recount
The fore-recited practices; whereof
We cannot feel too little, hear too much.

WOL. Stand forth, and with bold spirit relate what you,
Most like a careful subject, have collected   130
Out of the Duke of Buckingham.
    KING.   Speak freely.
    SURV. First, it was usual with him, every day
It would infect his speech, that if the king
Should without issue die, he 'll carry it so
To make the sceptre his: these very words
I 've heard him utter to his son-in-law,
Lord Abergavenny, to whom by oath he menaced
Revenge upon the cardinal.
    WOL.   Please your highness, note
This dangerous conception in this point.
Not friended by his wish, to your high person   140
His will is most malignant, and it stretches
Beyond you to your friends.
    Q. KATH.   My learn'd lord cardinal,
Deliver all with charity.
    KING.   Speak on:
How grounded he his title to the crown
Upon our fail? to this point hast thou heard him
At any time speak aught?
    SURV.   He was brought to this
By a vain prophecy of Nicholas Henton.
    KING. What was that Henton?
    SURV.   Sir, a Chartreux friar,
His confessor, who fed him every minute
With words of sovereignty.
    KING.   How know'st thou this?   150
    SURV. Not long before your highness sped to France,
The duke being at the Rose, within the parish
Saint Lawrence Poultney, did of me demand
What was the speech among the Londoners
Concerning the French journey: I replied,
Men fear'd the French would prove perfidious,
To the king's danger. Presently the duke
Said, 'twas the fear indeed, and that he doubted
'Twould prove the verity of certain words
Spoke by a holy monk; 'that oft,' says he,   160
'Hath sent to me, wishing me to permit
John de la Car, my chaplain, a choice hour
To hear from him a matter of some moment:

Whom after under the confession's seal
He solemnly had sworn, that what he spoke
My chaplain to no creature living but
To me should utter, with demure confidence
This pausingly ensued: Neither the king nor 's heirs,
Tell you the duke, shall prosper: bid him strive
To gain the love o' the commonalty: the duke   170
Shall govern England.'

     Q. KATH.   If I know you well,
You were the duke's surveyor and lost your office
On the complaint o' the tenants: take good heed
You charge not in your spleen a noble person
And spoil your nobler soul: I say, take heed;
Yes, heartily beseech you.

     KING.   Let him on.
Go forward.

     SURV.   On my soul, I'll speak but truth.
I told my lord the duke, by the devil's illusions
The monk might be deceived; and that 'twas dangerous for him
To ruminate on this so far, until   180
It forged him some design, which, being believed,
It was much like to do: he answer'd 'Tush,
It can do me no damage;' adding further,
That, had the king in his last sickness fail'd,
The cardinal's and Sir Thomas Lovell's heads
Should have gone off.

     KING.   Ha! what, so rank? Ah, ha!
There's mischief in this man: canst thou say further?

     SURV. I can, my liege.

     KING.   Proceed.

     SURV.   Being at Greenwich,
After your highness had reproved the duke
About Sir William Bulmer,—

     KING.   I remember   190
Of such a time: being my sworn servant,
The duke retain'd him his. But on; what hence?

     SURV. 'If' quoth he 'I for this had been committed,
As to the Tower I thought, I would have play'd
The part my father meant to act upon
The usurper Richard; who, being at Salisbury,
Made suit to come in 's presence; which if granted,
As he made semblance of his duty, would

Have put his knife into him.'

 KING.   A giant traitor!

 WOL. Now, madam, may his highness live in freedom,   200
And this man out of prison?

 Q. KATH.   God mend all!

 KING. There's something more would out of thee; what say'st?

 SURV. After 'the duke his father,' with the 'knife,'
He stretch'd him, and with one hand on his dagger,
Another spread on 's breast, mounting his eyes,
He did discharge a horrible oath, whose tenour
Was, were he evil used, he would outgo
His father by as much as a performance
Does an irresolute purpose.

 KING.   There 's his period,
To sheathe his knife in us. He is attach'd;   210
Call him to present trial: if he may
Find mercy in the law, 'tis his; if none,
Let him not seek 't of us: by day and night!
He 's traitor to the height.   [*Exeunt.*

SCENE III. *An Ante-Chamber in the Palace.*

Enter the LORD CHAMBERLAIN *and* LORD SANDS.

 CHAM. Is 't possible the spells of France should juggle
Men into such strange mysteries?

 SANDS.   New customs,
Though they be never so ridiculous,
Nay, let 'em be unmanly, yet are follow'd.

 CHAM. As far as I see, all the good our English
Have got by the late voyage is but merely
A fit or two o' the face; but they are shrewd ones;
For when they hold 'em, you would swear directly
Their very noses had been counsellors
To Pepin or Clotharius, they keep state so.   10

 SANDS. They have all new legs, and lame ones: one would
    take it,

That never saw 'em pace before, the spavin
Or springhalt reign'd among 'em.
    CHAM.   Death! my lord,
Their clothes are after such a pagan cut too,
That, sure, they've worn out Christendom.

Enter SIR THOMAS LOVELL.

                                       How now!

What news, Sir Thomas Lovell?
    LOV.   Faith, my lord,
I hear of none but the new proclamation
That 's clapp'd upon the court-gate.
    CHAM.   What is 't for?
    LOV. The reformation of our travell'd gallants,
That fill the court with quarrels, talk, and tailors.   20
    CHAM. I 'm glad 'tis there: now I would pray our monsieurs
To think an English courtier may be wise,
And never see the Louvre.
    LOV.   They must either,
For so run the conditions, leave those remnants
Of fool and feather that they got in France,
With all their honourable points of ignorance
Pertaining thereunto, as fights and fireworks,
Abusing better men than they can be
Out of a foreign wisdom, renouncing clean
The faith they have in tennis and tall stockings,   30
Short blister'd breeches and those types of travel,
And understand again like honest men,
Or pack to their old playfellows: there, I take it,
They may, 'cum privilegio,' wear away
The lag end of their lewdness, and be laugh'd at.
    SANDS. 'Tis time to give 'em physic, their diseases
Are grown so catching.
    CHAM.   What a loss our ladies
Will have of these trim vanities!
    LOV.   Ay, marry,
There will be woe indeed, lords: the sly whoresons
Have got a speeding trick to lay down ladies;   40
A French song and a fiddle has no fellow.
    SANDS. The devil fiddle 'em! I am glad they are going,

For, sure, there 's no converting of 'em: now
An honest country lord, as I am, beaten
A long time out of play, may bring his plain-song,
And have an hour of hearing; and, by'r lady,
Held current music too.

CHAM.   Well said, Lord Sands;
Your colt's tooth is not cast yet.

SANDS.   No, my lord;
Nor shall not, while I have a stump.

CHAM.   Sir Thomas,
Whither were you a-going?

LOV.   To the cardinal's: 50
Your lordship is a guest too.

CHAM.   O, 'tis true:
This night he makes a supper, and a great one,
To many lords and ladies; there will be
The beauty of this kingdom, I 'll assure you.

LOV. That churchman bears a bounteous mind indeed,
A hand as fruitful as the land that feeds us;
His dews fall every where.

CHAM.   No doubt he 's noble;
He had a black mouth that said other of him.

SANDS. He may, my lord; has wherewithal: in him
Sparing would show a worse sin than ill doctrine: 60
Men of his way should be most liberal;
They are set here for examples.

CHAM.   True, they are so;
But few now give so great ones. My barge stays;
Your lordship shall along. Come, good Sir Thomas,
We shall be late else; which I would not be,
For I was spoke to, with Sir Henry Guildford
This night to be comptrollers.

SANDS.   I am your lordship's.   [*Exeunt.*

SCENE IV. *A Hall in York Place.*

Hautboys. A small table under a state for the CARDINAL, *a longer table
for the guests. Then enter* ANNE BULLEN *and divers other* Ladies
and Gentlemen *as guests, at one door; at another door, enter* SIR
HENRY GUILDFORD.

GUILD. Ladies, a general welcome from his grace
Salutes ye all; this night he dedicates
To fair content and you: none here, he hopes,
In all this noble bevy, has brought with her
One care abroad; he would have all as merry
As, first, good company, good wine, good welcome,
Can make good people.

Enter LORD CHAMBERLAIN, LORD SANDS, *and* SIR THOMAS
LOVELL.

         O, my lord, you 're tardy:
The very thought of this fair company
Clapp'd wings to me.
  CHAM.   You are young, Sir Harry Guildford.
  SANDS. Sir Thomas Lovell, had the cardinal   10
But half my lay thoughts in him, some of these
Should find a running banquet ere they rested,
I think would better please 'em: by my life,
They are a sweet society of fair ones.
  LOV. O, that your lordship were but now confessor
To one or two of these!
  SANDS.   I would I were;
They should find easy penance.
  LOV.   Faith, how easy?
  SANDS. As easy as a down-bed would afford it.
  CHAM. Sweet ladies, will it please you sit? Sir Harry,
Place you that side; I 'll take the charge of this: 20
His grace is entering. Nay, you must not freeze;
Two women placed together makes cold weather:
My Lord Sands, you are one will keep 'em waking;
Pray, sit between these ladies.
  SANDS.   By my faith,
And thank your lordship. By your leave, sweet ladies:
If I chance to talk a little wild, forgive me;
I had it from my father.
  ANNE.   Was he mad, sir?
  SANDS. O, very mad, exceeding mad, in love too:
But he would bite none; just as I do now,
He would kiss you twenty with a breath.   [*Kisses her.*
  CHAM.   Well said, my lord.   30
So, now you 're fairly seated. Gentlemen,

The penance lies on you, if these fair ladies
Pass away frowning.

SANDS.   For my little cure,
Let me alone.

Hautboys. Enter CARDINAL WOLSEY, *and takes his state.*

WOL. You 're welcome, my fair guests: that noble lady
Or gentleman that is not freely merry,
Is not my friend: this, to confirm my welcome;
And to you all, good health.   [*Drinks.*

SANDS.   Your grace is noble:
Let me have such a bowl may hold my thanks,
And save me so much talking.

WOL.   My Lord Sands,   40
I am beholding to you: cheer your neighbours.
Ladies, you are not merry: gentlemen,
Whose fault is this?

SANDS.   The red wine first must rise
In their fair cheeks, my lord; then we shall have 'em
Talk us to silence.

ANNE.   You are a merry gamester,
My Lord Sands.

SANDS.   Yes, if I make my play.
Here 's to your ladyship: and pledge it, madam,
For 'tis to such a thing—

ANNE.   You cannot show me.

SANDS. I told your grace they would talk anon.
                    [*Drum and trumpet: chambers discharged.*

WOL.   What's that?

CHAM. Look out there, some of ye.   [*Exit Servant.*

WOL.   What warlike voice,   50
And to what end, is this? Nay, ladies, fear not;
By all the laws of war you 're privileged.

Re-enter Servant.

CHAM. How now! what is 't?

SERV.   A noble troop of strangers;
For so they seem: they 've left their barge, and landed;
And hither make, as great ambassadors

From foreign princes.
  Wol.   Good lord chamberlain,
Go, give 'em welcome; you can speak the French tongue;
And, pray, receive 'em nobly and conduct 'em
Into our presence, where this heaven of beauty
Shall shine at full upon them. Some attend him.   60
       [*Exit Chamberlain, attended. All rise, and tables removed.*
You have now a broken banquet; but we 'll mend it.
A good digestion to you all: and once more
I shower a welcome on ye; welcome all.

Hautboys. Enter the King *and others, as masquers, habited like shepherds,*
    ushered by the Lord Chamberlain. *They pass directly before the*
    Cardinal, *and gracefully salute him.*

A noble company! what are their pleasures?
  Cham. Because they speak no English, thus they pray'd
To tell your grace, that, having heard by fame
Of this so noble and so fair assembly
This night to meet here, they could do no less,
Out of the great respect they bear to beauty,
But leave their flocks, and under your fair conduct   70
Crave leave to view these ladies and entreat
An hour of revels with 'em.
  Wol.   Say, lord chamberlain,
They have done my poor house grace; for which I pay 'em
A thousand thanks and pray 'em take their pleasures.
        [*They choose. The King chooses Anne Bullen.*
  King. The fairest hand I ever touch'd! O beauty,
Till now I never knew thee!   [*Music. Dance.*
  Wol. My lord!
  Cham.   Your grace?
  Wol.   Pray, tell 'em thus much from me:
There should be one amongst 'em, by his person,
More worthy this place than myself; to whom,
If I but knew him, with my love and duty   80
I would surrender it.
  Cham.   I will, my lord.   [*Whispers the Masquers.*
  Wol. What say they?
  Cham.   Such a one, they all confess,
There is indeed; which they would have your grace

Find out, and he will take it.

WOL.   Let me see then.
By all your good leaves, gentlemen; here I 'll make
My royal choice.

KING.   [*Unmasking*] Ye have found him, cardinal:
You hold a fair assembly; you do well, lord:
You are a churchman, or, I' ll tell you, cardinal,
I should judge now unhappily.

WOL.   I am glad
Your grace is grown so pleasant.

KING.   My lord chamberlain,   90
Prithee, come hither: what fair lady's that?

CHAM. An 't please your grace, Sir Thomas Bullen's daughter,
The Viscount Rochford, one of her highness' women.

KING. By heaven, she is a dainty one. Sweetheart,
I were unmannerly, to take you out,
And not to kiss you. A health, gentlemen!
Let it go round.

WOL. Sir Thomas Lovell, is the banquet ready
I' the privy chamber?

LOV.   Yes, my lord.

WOL.   Your grace,
I fear, with dancing is a little heated.   100

KING. I fear, too much.

WOL.   There's fresher air, my lord,
In the next chamber.

KING. Lead in your ladies, every one. Sweet partner,
I must not yet forsake you. Let's be merry,
Good my lord cardinal: I have half a dozen healths
To drink to these fair ladies, and a measure
To lead 'em once again; and then let's dream
Who 's best in favour. Let the music knock it.

                              [*Exeunt with trumpets.*

ACT II.

Scene I. *Westminster. A Street.*

Enter two Gentlemen, *meeting.*

First Gent. Whither away so fast?

Sec. Gent.   O, God save ye!
Even to the hall, to hear what shall become
Of the great Duke of Buckingham.

First Gent.   I 'll save you
That labour, sir. All 's now done, but the ceremony
Of bringing back the prisoner.

Sec. Gent.   Were you there?

First Gent. Yes, indeed was I.

Sec. Gent.   Pray, speak what has happen'd.

First Gent. You may guess quickly what.

Sec. Gent.   Is he found guilty?

First Gent. Yes, truly is he, and condemn'd upon 't.

Sec. Gent. I am sorry for 't.

First Gent.   So are a number more.

Sec. Gent. But, pray, how pass'd it?   10

First Gent. I'll tell you in a little. The great duke
Came to the bar; where to his accusations
He pleaded still not guilty, and alleged
Many sharp reasons to defeat the law.
The king's attorney on the contrary
Urged on the examinations, proofs, confessions
Of divers witnesses; which the duke desired
To have brought viva voce to his face:
At which appear'd against him his surveyor;
Sir Gilbert Peck his chancellor; and John Car,   20
Confessor to him; with that devil monk,
Hopkins, that made this mischief.

Sec. Gent.   That was he
That fed him with his prophecies?

First Gent.   The same.
All these accused him strongly; which he fain
Would have flung from him, but indeed he could not:
And so his peers upon this evidence
Have found him guilty of high treason. Much

He spoke, and learnedly, for life, but all
Was either pitied in him or forgotten.

    SEC. GENT. After all this, how did he bear himself? 30
    FIRST GENT. When he was brought again to the bar, to hear
His knell rung out, his judgement, he was stirr'd
With such an agony, he sweat extremely,
And something spoke in choler, ill and hasty:
But he fell to himself again and sweetly
In all the rest show'd a most noble patience.

    SEC. GENT. I do not think he fears death.
    FIRST GENT.   Sure, he does not;
He never was so womanish; the cause
He may a little grieve at.

    SEC. GENT.   Certainly
The cardinal is the end of this.

    FIRST GENT.   'Tis likely, 40
By all conjectures: first, Kildare's attainder,
Then deputy of Ireland; who removed,
Earl Surrey was sent thither, and in haste too,
Lest he should help his father.

    SEC. GENT.   That trick of state
Was a deep envious one.

    FIRST GENT.   At his return
No doubt he will requite it. This is noted,
And generally, whoever the king favours,
The cardinal instantly will find employment,
And far enough from court too.

    SEC. GENT.   All the commons
Hate him perniciously, and, o' my conscience, 50
Wish him ten fathom deep: this duke as much
They love and dote on; call him bounteous Buckingham,
The mirror of all courtesy—

    FIRST GENT.   Stay there, sir,
And see the noble ruin'd man you speak of.

Enter BUCKINGHAM *from his arraignment, tipstaves before him, the axe
    with the edge towards him, halberds on each side, accompanied with*
    SIR THOMAS LOVELL, SIR NICHOLAS VAUX, SIR WILLIAM
    SANDS, *and common people, &c.*

    SEC. GENT. Let's stand close, and behold him.
    BUCK.   All good people,

You that thus far have come to pity me,
Hear what I say, and then go home and lose me.
I have this day received a traitor's judgement,
And by that name must die: yet, heaven bear witness,
And if I have a conscience, let it sink me, 60
Even as the axe falls, if I be not faithful!
The law I bear no malice for my death;
'T has done upon the premises but justice:
But those that sought it I could wish more Christians:
Be what they will, I heartily forgive 'em:
Yet let 'em look they glory not in mischief,
Nor build their evils on the graves of great men;
For then my guiltless blood must cry against 'em.
For further life in this world I ne'er hope,
Nor will I sue, although the king have mercies 70
More than I dare make faults. You few that loved me
And dare be bold to weep for Buckingham,
His noble friends and fellows, whom to leave
Is only bitter to him, only dying,
Go with me, like good angels, to my end,
And, as the long divorce of steel falls on me,
Make of your prayers one sweet sacrifice
And lift my soul to heaven. Lead on, o' God's name.
  Lov. I do beseech your grace, for charity,
If ever any malice in your heart 80
Were hid against me, now to forgive me frankly.
  Buck. Sir Thomas Lovell, I as free forgive you
As I would be forgiven: I forgive all;
There cannot be those numberless offences
'Gainst me, that I cannot take peace with: no black envy
Shall mark my grave. Commend me to his grace,
And if he speak of Buckingham, pray tell him
You met him half in heaven: my vows and prayers
Yet are the king's, and, till my soul forsake,
Shall cry for blessings on him: may he live 90
Longer than I have time to tell his years!
Ever beloved and loving may his rule be!
And when old time shall lead him to his end,
Goodness and he fill up one monument!
  Lov. To the water side I must conduct your grace;
Then give my charge up to Sir Nicholas Vaux,
Who undertakes you to your end.

VAUX.   Prepare there;
The duke is coming: see the barge be ready,
And fit it with such furniture as suits
The greatness of his person.
BUCK.   Nay, Sir Nicholas,   100
Let it alone; my state now will but mock me.
When I came hither, I was lord high constable
And Duke of Buckingham; now, poor Edward Bohun:
Yet I am richer than my base accusers,
That never knew what truth meant: I now seal it;
And with that blood will make 'em one day groan for 't.
My noble father, Henry of Buckingham,
Who first raised head against usurping Richard,
Flying for succour to his servant Banister,
Being distress'd, was by that wretch betray'd,   110
And without trial fell; God's peace be with him!
Henry the Seventh succeeding, truly pitying
My father's loss, like a most royal prince,
Restored me to my honours, and out of ruins
Made my name once more noble. Now his son,
Henry the Eighth, life, honour, name and all
That made me happy, at one stroke has taken
For ever from the world. I had my trial,
And must needs say, a noble one; which makes me
A little happier than my wretched father: 120
Yet thus far we are one in fortunes: both
Fell by our servants, by those men we loved most;
A most unnatural and faithless service!
Heaven has an end in all: yet, you that hear me,
This from a dying man receive as certain:
Where you are liberal of your loves and counsels
Be sure you be not loose; for those you make friends
And give your hearts to, when they once perceive
The least rub in your fortunes, fall away
Like water from ye, never found again   130
But where they mean to sink ye. All good people,
Pray for me! I must now forsake ye: the last hour
Of my long weary life is come upon me.
Farewell:
And when you would say something that is sad,

Speak how I fell. I have done; and God forgive me!

                                [Exeunt Duke and Train.

    FIRST GENT. O, this is full of pity! Sir, it calls,
I fear, too many curses on their heads
That were the authors.

    SEC. GENT.   If the duke be guiltless,
'Tis full of woe: yet I can give you inkling   140
Of an ensuing evil, if it fall,
Greater than this.

    FIRST GENT.   Good angels keep it from us!
What may it be? You do not doubt my faith, sir?

    SEC. GENT. This secret is so weighty, 'twill require
A strong faith to conceal it.

    FIRST GENT.   Let me have it;
I do not talk much.

    SEC. GENT.   I am confident;
You shall, sir: did you not of late days hear
A buzzing of a separation
Between the king and Katharine?

    FIRST GENT.   Yes, but it held not:
For when the king once heard it, out of anger   150
He sent command to the lord mayor straight
To stop the rumour and allay those tongues
That durst disperse it.

    SEC. GENT.   But that slander, sir,
Is found a truth now: for it grows again
Fresher than e'er it was, and held for certain
The king will venture at it. Either the cardinal,
Or some about him near, have, out of malice
To the good queen, possess'd him with a scruple
That will undo her: to confirm this too,
Cardinal Campeius is arrived, and lately;   160
As all think, for this business.

    FIRST GENT.   'Tis the cardinal;
And merely to revenge him on the emperor,
For not bestowing on him at his asking
The archbishopric of Toledo, this is purposed.

    SEC. GENT. I think you have hit the mark: but is 't not cruel
That she should feel the smart of this? The cardinal
Will have his will, and she must fall.

First Gent. 'Tis woeful.
We are too open here to argue this;
Let 's think in private more. [*Exeunt.*

Scene II. *An Ante-Chamber in the Palace.*

Enter the Lord Chamberlain, *reading a letter.*

Cham. 'My lord, the horses your lordship sent for, with all the care
I had, I saw well chosen, ridden, and furnished. They were young and
handsome, and of the best breed in the north. When they were ready
to set out for London, a man of my lord cardinal's, by commission and
main power, took 'em from me; with this reason: His master would be
served before a subject, if not before the king; which stopped our mouths,
sir.'

I fear he will indeed: well, let him have them:
He will have all, I think.

Enter to the Lord Chamberlain, *the* Dukes of Norfolk
and Suffolk.

Nor. Well met, my lord chamberlain. 10
Cham. Good day to both your graces.
Suf. How is the king employ'd?
Cham. I left him private,
Full of sad thoughts and troubles.
Nor. What's the cause?
Cham. It seems the marriage with his brother's wife
Has crept too near his conscience.
Suf. No, his conscience
Has crept too near another lady.
Nor. 'Tis so:
This is the cardinal's doing, the king-cardinal:
That blind priest, like the eldest son of fortune,
Turns what he list. The king will know him one day.
Suf. Pray God he do! he 'll never know himself else. 20
Nor. How holily he works in all his business!

And with what zeal! for, now he has crack'd the league
Between us and the emperor, the queen's great nephew,
He dives into the king's soul, and there scatters
Dangers, doubts, wringing of the conscience,
Fears and despairs; and all these for his marriage:
And out of all these to restore the king,
He counsels a divorce; a loss of her
That, like a jewel, has hung twenty years
About his neck, yet never lost her lustre,   30
Of her that loves him with that excellence
That angels love good men with, even of her
That, when the greatest stroke of fortune falls,
Will bless the king: and is not this course pious?
    CHAM. Heaven keep me from such counsel! 'Tis most true
These news are every where; every tongue speaks 'em.
And every true heart weeps for 't: all that dare
Look into these affairs see this main end,
The French king's sister. Heaven will one day open
The king's eyes, that so long have slept upon   40
This bold bad man.
    SUF.   And free us from his slavery.
    NOR. We had need pray,
And heartily, for our deliverance;
Or this imperious man will work us all
From princes into pages: all men's honours
Lie like one lump before him, to be fashion'd
Into what pitch he please.
    SUF.   For me, my lords,
I love him not, nor fear him; there 's my creed:
As I am made without him, so I 'll stand,
If the king please; his curses and his blessings   50
Touch me alike; they're breath I not believe in.
I knew him, and I know him; so I leave him
To him that made him proud, the pope.
    NOR.   Let 's in;
And with some other business put the king
From these sad thoughts that work too much upon him:
My lord, you 'll bear us company?
    CHAM.   Excuse me;
The king has sent me otherwhere: besides,
You 'll find a most unfit time to disturb him:

Health to your lordships.

NOR.   Thanks, my good lord chamberlain.

[*Exit Lord Chamberlain; and the King draws
the curtain and sits reading pensively.*

SUF. How sad he looks! sure, he is much afflicted.   60

KING. Who 's there, ha?

NOR.   Pray God he be not angry.

KING. Who 's there, I say? How dare you thrust yourselves
Into my private meditations?
Who am I? ha?

NOR. A gracious king that pardons all offences
Malice ne'er meant: our breach of duty this way
Is business of estate, in which we come
To know your royal pleasure.

KING.   Ye are too bold:
Go to; I 'll make ye know your times of business:
Is this an hour for temporal affairs, ha?   70

Enter WOLSEY *and* CAMPEIUS, *with a commission.*

Who 's there? my good lord cardinal? O my Wolsey,
The quiet of my wounded conscience,
Thou art a cure fit for a king. [*To Camp.*] You 're welcome,
Most learned reverend sir, into our kingdom:
Use us and it. [*To Wols.*] My good lord, have great care
I be not found a talker.

WOL.   Sir, you cannot.
I would your grace would give us but an hour
Of private conference.

KING.   [*To For. and Suf.*] We are busy; go.

NOR. [*Aside to Suf.*] This priest has no pride in him?

SUF.   [*Aside to Nor.*] Not to speak of:
I would not be so sick though for his place: 80
But this cannot continue.

NOR.   [*Aside to Suf.*] If it do,
I 'll venture one have-at-him.

SUF.   [*Aside to Nor.*] I another.

[*Exeunt Norfolk and Suffolk.*

WOL. Your grace has given a precedent of wisdom
Above all princes, in committing freely
Your scruple to the voice of Christendom:

Who can be angry now? what envy reach you?
The Spaniard, tied by blood and favour to her,
Must now confess, if they have any goodness,
The trial just and noble. All the clerks,
I mean the learned ones, in Christian kingdoms   90
Have their free voices: Rome, the nurse of judgement,
Invited by your noble self, hath sent
One general tongue unto us, this good man,
This just and learned priest, Cardinal Campeius;
Whom once more I present unto your highness.

KING. And once more in mine arms I bid him welcome,
And thank the holy conclave for their loves:
They have sent me such a man I would have wish'd for.

CAM. Your grace must needs deserve all strangers' loves,
You are so noble. To your highness' hand   100
I tender my commission; by whose virtue,
The court of Rome commanding, you, my lord
Cardinal of York, are join'd with me their servant
In the unpartial judging of this business.

KING. Two equal men. The queen shall be acquainted
Forthwith for what you come. Where's Gardiner?

WOL. I know your majesty has always loved her
So dear in heart, not to deny her that
A woman of less place might ask by law,
Scholars allow'd freely to argue for her.   110

KING. Ay, and the best she shall have; and my favour
To him that does best: God forbid else. Cardinal,
Prithee, call Gardiner to me, my new secretary:
I find him a fit fellow.   [*Exit Wolsey.*

Re-enter WOLSEY, *with* GARDINER.

WOL. [*Aside to Gard.*] Give me your hand: much joy and favour
        to you:
You are the king's now.

GARD. [*Aside to Wol.*] But to be commanded
For ever by your grace, whose hand has raised me.

KING. Come hither, Gardiner.   [*Walks and whispers.*

CAM. My Lord of York, was not one Doctor Pace
In this man's place before him?

WOL.   Yes, he was.   120

CAM. Was he not held a learned man?
WOL.   Yes, surely.
CAM. Believe me, there 's an ill opinion spread then,
Even of yourself, lord cardinal.
WOL.   How! of me?
CAM. They will not stick to say you envied him,
And fearing he would rise, he was so virtuous,
Kept him a foreign man still; which so grieved him
That he ran mad and died.
WOL.   Heaven's peace be with him!
That 's Christian care enough: for living murmurers
There 's places of rebuke. He was a fool;
For he would needs be virtuous: that good fellow,   130
If I command him, follows my appointment:
I will have none so near else. Learn this, brother,
We live not to be griped by meaner persons.
    KING. Deliver this with modesty to the queen.
                                        [*Exit Gardiner.*

The most convenient place that I can think of
For such receipt of learning is Black-Friars;
There ye shall meet about this weighty business.
My Wolsey, see it furnish'd. O, my lord,
Would it not grieve an able man to leave
So sweet a bedfellow? But, conscience, conscience!   140
O, 'tis a tender place; and I must leave her.   [*Exeunt.*

SCENE III. *An Ante-Chamber of the Queen's Apartments.*

Enter ANNE BULLEN *and an old* Lady.

    ANNE. Not for that neither: here 's the pang that pinches:
His highness having lived so long with her, and she
So good a lady that no tongue could ever
Pronounce dishonour of her—by my life,
She never knew harm-doing—O, now, after
So many courses of the sun enthroned,
Still growing in a majesty and pomp, the which

To leave a thousand-fold more bitter than
'Tis sweet at first to acquire—after this process,
To give her the avaunt! it is a pity   10
Would move a monster.

   OLD L.   Hearts of most hard temper
Melt and lament for her.

   ANNE.   O, God's will! much better
She ne'er had known pomp: though 't be temporal,
Yet, if that quarrel, fortune, do divorce
It from the bearer, 'tis a sufferance panging
As soul and body's severing.

   OLD L.   Alas, poor lady!
She's a stranger now again.

   ANNE.   So much the more
Must pity drop upon her. Verily,
I swear, 'tis better to be lowly born,
And range with humble livers in content,   20
Than to be perk'd up in a glistering grief
And wear a golden sorrow.

   OLD L.   Our content
Is our best having.

   ANNE.   By my troth and maidenhead,
I would not be a queen.

   OLD L.   Beshrew me, I would,
And venture maidenhead for 't; and so would you,
For all this spice of your hypocrisy:
You, that have so fair parts of woman on you,
Have too a woman's heart; which ever yet
Affected eminence, wealth, sovereignty;
Which, to say sooth, are blessings; and which gifts—   30
Saving your mincing—the capacity
Of your soft cheveril conscience would receive,
If you might please to stretch it.

   ANNE.   Nay, good troth.

   OLD L. Yes, troth, and troth; you would not be a queen?

   ANNE. No, not for all the riches under heaven.

   OLD L. 'Tis strange: a three-pence bow'd would hire me,
Old as I am, to queen it: but, I pray you,
What think you of a duchess? have you limbs
To bear that load of title?

   ANNE.   No, in truth.

OLD L. Then you are weakly made: pluck off a little; 40
I would not be a young count in your way,
For more than blushing comes to: if your back
Cannot vouchsafe this burthen, 'tis too weak
Ever to get a boy.

ANNE.   How you do talk!
I swear again, I would not be a queen
For all the world.

OLD L. In faith, for little England
You 'ld venture an emballing: I myself
Would for Carnarvonshire, although there 'long'd
No more to the crown but that. Lo, who comes here?

Enter the LORD CHAMBERLAIN.

CHAM. Good morrow, ladies. What were 't worth to know 50
The secret of your conference?

ANNE.   My good lord,
Not your demand; it values not your asking:
Our mistress' sorrows we were pitying.

CHAM. It was a gentle business, and becoming
The action of good women: there is hope
All will be well.

ANNE. Now, I pray God, amen!

CHAM. You bear a gentle mind, and heavenly blessings
Follow such creatures. That you may, fair lady,
Perceive I speak sincerely, and high note 's
Ta'en of your many virtues, the king's majesty 60
Commends his good opinion of you, and
Does purpose honour to you no less flowing
Than Marchioness of Pembroke; to which title
A thousand pound a year, annual support,
Out of his grace he adds.

ANNE.   I do not know
What kind of my obedience I should tender;
More than my all is nothing: nor my prayers
Are not words duly hallowed, nor my wishes
More worth than empty vanities; yet prayers and wishes
Are all I can return. Beseech your lordship, 70
Vouchsafe to speak my thanks and my obedience,

As from a blushing handmaid, to his highness,
Whose health and royalty I pray for.

    CHAM.   Lady,
I shall not fail to approve the fair conceit
The king hath of you. [*Aside*] I have perused her well;
Beauty and honour in her are so mingled
That they have caught the king: and who knows yet
But from this lady may proceed a gem
To lighten all this isle?—I 'll to the king,
And say I spoke with you.

    ANNE.   My honour'd lord.   80

                        [*Exit Lord Chamberlain.*

    OLD L. Why, this it is; see, see!
I have been begging sixteen years in court,
Am yet a courtier beggarly, nor could
Come pat betwixt too early and too late
For any suit of pounds; and you, O fate!
A very fresh fish here—fie, fie, fie upon
This compell'd fortune!—have your mouth fill'd up
Before you open it.

    ANNE.   This is strange to me.

    OLD L. How tastes it? is it bitter? forty pence, no.
There was a lady once, 'tis an old story,   90
That would not be a queen, that would she not,
For all the mud in Egypt: have you heard it?

    ANNE. Come, you are pleasant.

    OLD L.   With your theme, I could
O'ermount the lark. The Marchioness of Pembroke!
A thousand pounds a year for pure respect!
No other obligation! By my life,
That promises mo thousands: honour's train
Is longer than his foreskirt. By this time
I know your back will bear a duchess: say,
Are you not stronger than you were?

    ANNE.   Good lady,   100
Make yourself mirth with your particular fancy,
And leave me out on 't. Would I had no being,
If this salute my blood a jot: it faints me,
To think what follows.
The queen is comfortless, and we forgetful

In our long absence: pray, do not deliver
What here you 've heard to her.
　　OLD L.　　　　　　　　　What do you think me?
　　　　　　　　　　　　　　　　　　　　[*Exeunt.*

SCENE IV. *A Hall in Black-Friars.*

Trumpets, sennet and cornets. Enter two Vergers, *with short silver
wands; next them, two* Scribes, *in the habit of doctors; after them,
the* ARCHBISHOP OF CANTERBURY *alone; after him, the* BISHOPS
OF LINCOLN, ELY, ROCHESTER, *and* Saint ASAPH; *next them,
with some small distance, follows a* Gentleman *bearing the purse,
with the great seal, and a cardinal's hat; then two* Priests, *bearing
each a silver cross; then a* Gentleman Usher *bare-headed,
accompanied with a* Sergeant at arms *bearing a silver mace; then
two* Gentlemen *bearing two great silver pillars; after them, side by
side, the two* CARDINALS; *two* Noblemen *with the sword and
mace. The* KING *takes place under the cloth of state; the two*
CARDINALS *sit under him as judges. The* QUEEN *takes place some
distance from the* KING. *The* BISHOPS *place themselves on each side
the court, in manner of a consistory; below them, the* Scribes. *The*
LORDS *sit next the* BISHOPS. *The rest of the* Attendants *stand in
convenient order about the stage.*

　　WOL. Whilst our commission from Rome is read,
Let silence be commanded.
　　KING.　　　　　　　　What 's the need?
It hath already publicly been read,
And on all sides the authority allow'd;
You may then spare that time.
　　WOL.　　　　　　　　　Be 't so. Proceed.
　　SCRIBE. Say, Henry King of England, come into the court.
　　CRIER. Henry King of England, &c.
　　KING. Here.
　　SCRIBE. Say, Katharine Queen of England, come into the court.
　　CRIER. Katharine Queen of England, &c.　　　　　　　　10
　　　　　　　　　　[*The Queen makes no answer, rises out of her
　　　　　　　　　　　　chair, goes about the court, comes to the
　　　　　　　　　　　　King, and kneels at his feet; then speaks.*

Q. KATH. Sir, I desire you do me right and justice,
And to bestow your pity on me; for
I am a most poor woman, and a stranger,
Born out of your dominions; having here
No judge indifferent, nor no more assurance
Of equal friendship and proceeding. Alas, sir,
In what have I offended you? what cause
Hath my behaviour given to your displeasure,
That thus you should proceed to put me off,
And take your good grace from me? Heaven witness,   20
I have been to you a true and humble wife,
At all times to your will conformable,
Ever in fear to kindle your dislike,
Yea, subject to your countenance, glad or sorry
As I saw it inclined: when was the hour
I ever contradicted your desire,
Or made it not mine too? Or which of your friends
Have I not strove to love, although I knew
He were mine enemy? what friend of mine
That had to him derived your anger, did I   30
Continue in my liking? nay, gave notice
He was from thence discharged? Sir, call to mind
That I have been your wife, in this obedience,
Upward of twenty years, and have been blest
With many children by you: if in the course
And process of this time you can report,
And prove it too, against mine honour aught,
My bond to wedlock or my love and duty,
Against your sacred person, in God's name,
Turn me away, and let the foul'st contempt   40
Shut door upon me, and so give me up
To the sharp'st kind of justice. Please you, sir,
The king, your father, was reputed for
A prince most prudent, of an excellent
And unmatch'd wit and judgement: Ferdinand,
My father, king of Spain, was reckon'd one
The wisest prince that there had reign'd by many
A year before: it is not to be question'd
That they had gather'd a wise council to them
Of every realm, that did debate this business,   50
Who deem'd our marriage lawful: wherefore I humbly

Beseech you, sir, to spare me, till I may
Be by my friends in Spain advised, whose counsel
I will implore: if not, i' the name of God,
Your pleasure be fulfill'd!

Wol.   You have here, lady,
And of your choice, these reverend fathers; men
Of singular integrity and learning,
Yea, the elect o' the land, who are assembled
To plead your cause: it shall be therefore bootless
That longer you desire the court, as well   60
For your own quiet, as to rectify
What is unsettled in the king.

Cam.   His grace
Hath spoken well and justly: therefore, madam,
It 's fit this royal session do proceed,
And that without delay their arguments
Be now produced and heard.

Q. Kath.   Lord cardinal,
To you I speak.

Wol.   Your pleasure, madam?

Q. Kath.   Sir,
I am about to weep; but, thinking that
We are a queen, or long have dream'd so, certain
The daughter of a king, my drops of tears   70
I 'll turn to sparks of fire.

Wol.   Be patient yet.

Q. Kath. I will, when you are humble; nay, before,
Or God will punish me. I do believe,
Induced by potent circumstances, that
You are mine enemy, and make my challenge
You shall not be my judge: for it is you
Have blown this coal betwixt my lord and me;
Which God's dew quench! Therefore I say again,
I utterly abhor, yea, from my soul
Refuse you for my judge; whom, yet once more,   80
I hold my most malicious foe, and think not
At all a friend to truth.

Wol.   I do profess
You speak not like yourself; who ever yet
Have stood to charity and display'd the effects
Of disposition gentle, and of wisdom

O'ertopping woman's power. Madam, you do me wrong:
I have no spleen against you, nor injustice
For you or any: how far I have proceeded,
Or how far further shall, is warranted
By a commission from the consistory,   90
Yea, the whole consistory of Rome. You charge me
That I have blown this coal: I do deny it:
The king is present: if it be known to him
That I gainsay my deed, how may he wound,
And worthily, my falsehood! yea, as much
As you have done my truth. If he know
That I am free of your report, he knows
I am not of your wrong. Therefore in him
It lies to cure me; and the cure is to
Remove these thoughts from you: the which before   100
His highness shall speak in, I do beseech
You, gracious madam, to unthink your speaking,
And to say so no more.
    Q. KATH.   My lord, my lord,
I am a simple woman, much too weak
To oppose your cunning. You're meek and humble-mouth'd;
You sign your place and calling, in full seeming,
With meekness and humility; but your heart
Is cramm'd with arrogancy, spleen, and pride.
You have, by fortune and his highness' favours,
Gone slightly o'er low steps, and now are mounted   110
Where powers are your retainers, and your words,
Domestics to you, serve your will as 't please
Yourself pronounce their office. I must tell you,
You tender more your person's honour than
Your high profession spiritual; that again
I do refuse you for my judge, and here,
Before you all, appeal unto the pope,
To bring my whole cause 'fore his holiness,
And to be judged by him.
               [*She curtsies to the King, and offers to depart.*
    CAM.   The queen is obstinate,
Stubborn to justice, apt to accuse it, and   120
Disdainful to be tried by 't: 'tis not well.
She's going away.
    KING. Call her again.

CRIER. Katharine Queen of England, come into the court.

GENT. USH. Madam, you are call'd back.

Q. KATH. What need you note it? pray you, keep your way:
When you are call'd, return. Now the Lord help!
They vex me past my patience. Pray you, pass on:
I will not tarry, no, nor ever more
Upon this business my appearance make   130
In any of their courts.   [*Exeunt Queen, and her Attendants.*

KING.   Go thy ways, Kate:
That man i' the world who shall report he has
A better wife, let him in nought be trusted,
For speaking false in that: thou art, alone,
If thy rare qualities, sweet gentleness,
Thy meekness saint-like, wife-like government,
Obeying in commanding, and thy parts
Sovereign and pious else, could speak thee out,
The queen of earthly queens. She's noble born,
And like her true nobility she has   140
Carried herself towards me.

WOL.   Most gracious sir,
In humblest manner I require your highness,
That it shall please you to declare in hearing
Of all these ears—for where I am robb'd and bound,
There must I be unloosed, although not there
At once and fully satisfied—whether ever I
Did broach this business to your highness, or
Laid any scruple in your way which might
Induce you to the question on 't? or ever
Have to you, but with thanks to God for such   150
A royal lady, spake one the least word that might
Be to the prejudice of her present state
Or touch of her good person?

KING.   My lord cardinal,
I do excuse you; yea, upon mine honour,
I free you from 't. You are not to be taught
That you have many enemies that know not
Why they are so, but, like to village curs,
Bark when their fellows do: by some of these
The queen is put in anger. You're excused:
But will you be more justified? you ever   160

Have wish'd the sleeping of this business, never desired
It to be stirr'd, but oft have hinder'd, oft,
The passages made toward it: on my honour,
I speak my good lord cardinal to this point,
And thus far clear him. Now, what moved me to 't,
I will be bold with time and your attention:
Then mark the inducement. Thus it came; give heed to 't:
My conscience first received a tenderness,
Scruple, and prick, on certain speeches utter'd
By the Bishop of Bayonne, then French ambassador;   170
Who had been hither sent on the debating
A marriage 'twixt the Duke of Orleans and
Our daughter Mary: i' the progress of this business,
Ere a determinate resolution, he,
I mean the bishop, did require a respite,
Wherein he might the king his lord advertise
Whether our daughter were legitimate,
Respecting this our marriage with the dowager,
Sometimes our brother's wife. This respite shook
The bosom of my conscience, enter'd me,   180
Yea, with a splitting power, and made to tremble
The region of my breast; which forced such way
That many mazed considerings did throng
And press'd in with this caution. First, methought
I stood not in the smile of heaven, who had
Commanded nature that my lady's womb,
If it conceived a male-child by me, should
Do no more offices of life to 't than
The grave does to the dead; for her male issue
Or died where they were made, or shortly after   190
This world had air'd them: hence I took a thought,
This was a judgement on me, that my kingdom,
Well worthy the best heir o' the world, should not
Be gladded in 't by me: then follows that
I weigh'd the danger which my realms stood in
By this my issue's fail; and that gave to me
Many a groaning throe. Thus hulling in
The wild sea of my conscience, I did steer
Toward this remedy whereupon we are
Now present here together; that's to say,   200

I meant to rectify my conscience, which
I then did feel full sick and yet not well,
By all the reverend fathers of the land
And doctors learn'd. First I began in private
With you, my Lord of Lincoln; you remember
How under my oppression I did reek,
When I first moved you.

LIN.   Very well, my liege.

KING. I have spoke long: be pleased yourself to say
How far you satisfied me.

LIN.   So please your highness,
The question did at first so stagger me,   210
Bearing a state of mighty moment in 't
And consequence of dread, that I committed
The daring'st counsel which I had to doubt,
And did entreat your highness to this course
Which you are running here.

KING.   I then moved you,
My Lord of Canterbury, and got your leave
To make this present summons: unsolicited
I left no reverend person in this court;
But by particular consent proceeded
Under your hands and seals: therefore, go on;   220
For no dislike i' the world against the person
Of the good queen, but the sharp thorny points
Of my alleged reasons, drive this forward:
Prove but our marriage lawful, by my life
And kingly dignity, we are contented
To wear our mortal state to come with her,
Katharine our queen, before the primest creature
That's paragon'd o' the world.

CAM.   So please your highness,
The queen being absent, 'tis a needful fitness
That we adjourn this court till further day: 230
Meanwhile must be an earnest motion
Made to the queen, to call back her appeal
She intends unto his holiness.

KING.   [*Aside*] I may perceive
These cardinals trifle with me: I abhor
This dilatory sloth and tricks of Rome.

My learn'd and well-beloved servant, Cranmer,
Prithee, return; with thy approach, I know,
My comfort comes along.—Break up the court:
I say, set on.

                    [*Exeunt in manner as they entered.*

ACT III.

SCENE I. *London. The Queen's Apartments.*

The QUEEN *and her* Women, *as at work.*

Q. KATH. Take thy lute, wench: my soul grows sad with troubles;
Sing, and disperse 'em, if thou canst: leave working.

SONG.

Orpheus with his lute made trees,
And the mountain tops that freeze,
    Bow themselves when he did sing:
To his music plants and flowers
Ever sprung, as sun and showers
    There had made a lasting spring.

Every thing that heard him play,
Even the billows of the sea,   10
    Hung their heads, and then lay by.
In sweet music is such art,
Killing care and grief of heart
    Fall asleep, or hearing die.

Enter a Gentleman.

Q. KATH. How now!
GENT. An 't please your grace, the two great cardinals
Wait in the presence.
Q. KATH.   Would they speak with me?
GENT. They will'd me say so, madam.
Q. KATH.   Pray their graces
To come near. [*Exit Gent.*] What can be their business
With me, a poor weak woman, fall'n from favour?   20
I do not like their coming. Now I think on 't,
They should be good men, their affairs as righteous:
But all hoods make not monks.

Enter the two CARDINALS, WOLSEY *and* CAMPEIUS.

WOL.   Peace to your highness!

44

Q. KATH. Your graces find me here part of a housewife;
I would be all, against the worst may happen.
What are your pleasures with me, reverend lords?

WOL. May it please you, noble madam, to withdraw
Into your private chamber, we shall give you
The full cause of our coming.

Q. KATH.   Speak it here;
There's nothing I have done yet, o' my conscience,   30
Deserves a corner: would all other women
Could speak this with as free a soul as I do!
My lords, I care not, so much I am happy
Above a number, if my actions
Were tried by every tongue, every eye saw 'em,
Envy and base opinion set against 'em,
I know my life so even. If your business
Seek me out, and that way I am wife in,
Out with it boldly: truth loves open dealing.

WOL. Tanta est erga te mentis integritas, regina serenissima,— 40
Q. KATH. O, good my lord, no Latin;
I am not such a truant since my coming,
As not to know the language I have lived in:
A strange tongue makes my cause more strange, suspicious;
Pray speak in English: here are some will thank you,
If you speak truth, for their poor mistress' sake;
Believe me, she has had much wrong: lord cardinal,
The willing'st sin I ever yet committed
May be absolved in English.

WOL.   Noble lady,
I am sorry my integrity should breed,   50
And service to his majesty and you,
So deep suspicion, where all faith was meant.
We come not by the way of accusation,
To taint that honour every good tongue blesses,
Nor to betray you any way to sorrow—
You have too much, good lady—but to know
How you stand minded in the weighty difference
Between the king and you, and to deliver,
Like free and honest men, our just opinions
And comforts to your cause.

CAM.   Most honour'd madam,   60
My Lord of York, out of his noble nature,

Zeal and obedience he still bore your grace,
Forgetting, like a good man, your late censure
Both of his truth and him, which was too far,
Offers, as I do, in a sign of peace,
His service and his counsel.

Q. KATH.   [*Aside*] To betray me.—
My lords, I thank you both for your good wills;
Ye speak like honest men; pray God, ye prove so!
But how to make ye suddenly an answer,
In such a point of weight, so near mine honour,   70
More near my life, I fear, with my weak wit,
And to such men of gravity and learning,
In truth, I know not. I was set at work
Among my maids, full little, God knows, looking
Either for such men or such business.
For her sake that I have been—for I feel
The last fit of my greatness—good your graces,
Let me have time and counsel for my cause:
Alas, I am a woman, friendless, hopeless!

WOL. Madam, you wrong the king's love with these fears: 80
Your hopes and friends are infinite.

Q. KATH.   In England
But little for my profit: can you think, lords,
That any Englishman dare give me counsel?
Or be a known friend, 'gainst his highness' pleasure—
Though he be grown so desperate to be honest—
And live a subject? Nay, forsooth, my friends,
They that must weigh out my afflictions,
They that my trust must grow to, live not here:
They are, as all my other comforts, far hence
In mine own country, lords.

CAM.   I would your grace   90
Would leave your griefs, and take my counsel.

Q. KATH.   How, sir?

CAM. Put your main cause into the king's protection;
He's loving and most gracious: 'twill be much
Both for your honour better and your cause;
For if the trial of the law o'ertake ye,
You 'll part away disgraced.

WOL.   He tells you rightly.

Q. KATH. Ye tell me what ye wish for both, my ruin:

Is this your Christian counsel? out upon ye!
Heaven is above all yet; there sits a judge
That no king can corrupt.
    CAM.   Your rage mistakes us.   100
    Q. KATH. The more shame for ye: holy men I thought ye,
Upon my soul, two reverend cardinal virtues;
But cardinal sins and hollow hearts I fear ye:
Mend 'em, for shame, my lords. Is this your comfort?
The cordial that ye bring a wretched lady,
A woman lost among ye, laugh'd at, scorn'd?
I will not wish ye half my miseries;
I have more charity: but say, I warn'd ye;
Take heed, for heaven's sake, take heed, lest at once
The burthen of my sorrows fall upon ye.   110
    WOL. Madam, this is a mere distraction;
You turn the good we offer into envy.
    Q. KATH. Ye turn me into nothing: woe upon ye,
And all such false professors! would you have me—
If you have any justice, any pity,
If ye be any thing but churchmen's habits—
Put my sick cause into his hands that hates me?
Alas, has banish'd me his bed already,
His love, too long ago! I am old, my lords,
And all the fellowship I hold now with him   120
Is only my obedience. What can happen
To me above this wretchedness? all your studies
Make me a curse like this.
    CAM.   Your fears are worse.
    Q. KATH. Have I lived thus long—let me speak myself,
Since virtue finds no friends—a wife, a true one?
A woman, I dare say without vain-glory,
Never yet branded with suspicion?
Have I with all my full affections
Still met the king? loved him next heaven? obey'd him?
Been, out of fondness, superstitious to him?   130
Almost forgot my prayers to content him?
And am I thus rewarded? 'tis not well, lords.
Bring me a constant woman to her husband,
One that ne'er dream'd a joy beyond his pleasure,
And to that woman, when she has done most,
Yet will I add an honour, a great patience.

WOL. Madam, you wander from the good we aim at.

Q. KATH. My lord, I dare not make myself so guilty,
To give up willingly that noble title
Your master wed me to: nothing but death   140
Shall e'er divorce my dignities.

WOL.   Pray, hear me.

Q. KATH. Would I had never trod this English earth,
Or felt the flatteries that grow upon it!
Ye have angels' faces, but heaven knows your hearts.
What will become of me now, wretched lady!
I am the most unhappy woman living.
Alas, poor wenches, where are now your fortunes?
Shipwreck'd upon a kingdom, where no pity,
No friends, no hope; no kindred weep for me;
Almost no grave allow'd me: like the lily,   150
That once was mistress of the field and flourish'd,
I 'll hang my head and perish.

WOL.   If your grace
Could but be brought to know our ends are honest,
You 'ld feel more comfort: why should we, good lady,
Upon what cause, wrong you? alas, our places,
The way of our profession is against it:
We are to cure such sorrows, not to sow 'em.
For goodness' sake, consider what you do;
How you may hurt yourself, ay, utterly
Grow from the king's acquaintance, by this carriage.   160
The hearts of princes kiss obedience,
So much they love it; but to stubborn spirits
They swell, and grow as terrible as storms.
I know you have a gentle, noble temper,
A soul as even as a calm: pray think us
Those we profess, peace-makers, friends and servants.

CAM. Madam, you'll find it so. You wrong your virtues
With these weak women's fears: a noble spirit,
As yours was put into you, ever casts
Such doubts, as false coin, from it. The king loves you;   170
Beware you lose it not: for us, if you please
To trust us in your business, we are ready
To use our utmost studies in your service.

Q. KATH. Do what ye will, my lords: and pray forgive me,
If I have used myself unmannerly;

You know I am a woman, lacking wit
To make a seemly answer to such persons.
Pray do my service to his majesty:
He has my heart yet, and shall have my prayers
While I shall have my life. Come, reverend fathers,   180
Bestow your counsels on me: she now begs,
That little thought, when she set footing here,
She should have bought her dignities so dear.   [*Exeunt.*

Scene II. *Ante-Chamber to the King's Apartment.*

Enter the Duke of Norfolk, *the* Duke of Suffolk, *the* Earl of Surrey, *and the* Lord Chamberlain.

Nor. If you will now unite in your complaints
And force them with a constancy, the cardinal
Cannot stand under them: if you omit
The offer of this time, I cannot promise
But that you shall sustain moe new disgraces,
With these you bear already.

Sur.   I am joyful
To meet the least occasion that may give me
Remembrance of my father-in-law, the duke,
To be revenged on him.

Suf.   Which of the peers
Have uncontemn'd gone by him, or at least   10
Strangely neglected? when did he regard
The stamp of nobleness in any person
Out of himself?

Cham.   My lords, you speak your pleasures:
What he deserves of you and me I know;
What we can do to him, though now the time
Gives way to us, I much fear. If you cannot
Bar his access to the king, never attempt
Any thing on him; for he hath a witchcraft
Over the king in 's tongue.

Nor.   O, fear him not;

His spell in that is out: the king hath found   20
Matter against him that for ever mars
The honey of his language. No, he's settled,
Not to come off, in his displeasure.

    Sur.   Sir,
I should be glad to hear such news as this
Once every hour.

    Nor.   Believe it, this is true:
In the divorce his contrary proceedings
Are all unfolded; wherein he appears
As I would wish mine enemy.

    Sur.   How came
His practices to light?

    Suf.   Most strangely.

    Sur.   O, how, how?

    Suf. The cardinal's letters to the pope miscarried,   30
And came to the eye o' the king: wherein was read
How that the cardinal did entreat his holiness
To stay the judgement o' the divorce; for if
It did take place, 'I do' quoth he 'perceive
My king is tangled in affection to
A creature of the queen's, Lady Anne Bullen.'

    Sur. Has the king this?

    Suf.   Believe it.

    Sur.   Will this work?

    Cham. The king in this perceives him, how he coasts
And hedges his own way. But in this point
All his tricks founder, and he brings his physic   40
After his patient's death: the king already
Hath married the fair lady.

    Sur.   Would he had!

    Suf. May you be happy in your wish, my lord!
For, I profess, you have it.

    Sur.   Now, all my joy
Trace the conjunction!

    Suf.   My amen to 't!

    Nor.   All men's!

    Suf. There 's order given for her coronation:
Marry, this is yet but young, and may be left
To some ears unrecounted. But, my lords,
She is a gallant creature and complete

In mind and feature: I persuade me, from her   50
Will fall some blessing to this land, which shall
In it be memorized.

    SUR.   But will the king
Digest this letter of the cardinal's?
The Lord forbid!

    NOR.   Marry, amen!

    SUF.   No, no;
There be moe wasps that buzz about his nose
Will make this sting the sooner. Cardinal Campeius
Is stol'n away to Rome; hath ta'en no leave;
Has left the cause o' the king unhandled, and
Is posted as the agent of our cardinal,
To second all his plot. I do assure you   60
The king cried 'Ha!' at this.

    CHAM.   Now God incense him,
And let him cry 'Ha!' louder!

    NOR.   But, my lord,
When returns Cranmer?

    SUF. He is return'd in his opinions, which
Have satisfied the king for his divorce,
Together with all famous colleges
Almost in Christendom: shortly, I believe,
His second marriage shall be publish'd, and
Her coronation. Katharine no more
Shall be call'd queen, but princess dowager   70
And widow to Prince Arthur.

    NOR.   This same Cranmer's
A worthy fellow, and hath ta'en much pain
In the king's business.

    SUF.   He has; and we shall see him
For it an archbishop.

    NOR.   So I hear.

    SUF.   'Tis so.
The cardinal!

Enter WOLSEY *and* CROMWELL.

    NOR.   Observe, observe, he's moody.

    WOL. The packet, Cromwell,
Gave 't you the king?

CROM.   To his own hand, in 's bedchamber.

WOL. Look'd he o' the inside of the paper?

CROM.   Presently
He did unseal them, and the first he view'd,
He did it with a serious mind; a heed   80
Was in his countenance. You he bade
Attend him here this morning.

WOL.   Is he ready
To come abroad?

CROM.   I think, by this he is.

WOL. Leave me awhile.   [*Exit Cromwell.*
[*Aside*] It shall be to the Duchess of Alençon,
The French king's sister: he shall marry her.
Anne Bullen! No; I'll no Anne Bullens for him:
There's more in 't than fair visage. Bullen!
No, we'll no Bullens. Speedily I wish
To hear from Rome. The Marchioness of Pembroke!   90

NOR. He's discontented.

SUF.   May be, he hears the king
Does whet his anger to him.

SUR.   Sharp enough,
Lord, for thy justice!

WOL. [*Aside*] The late queen's gentlewoman, a knight's daughter,
To be her mistress' mistress! the queen's queen!
This candle burns not clear: 'tis I must snuff it;
Then out it goes. What though I know her virtuous
And well deserving? yet I know her for
A spleeny Lutheran, and not wholesome to
Our cause, that she should lie i' the bosom of   100
Our hard-ruled king. Again, there is sprung up
An heretic, an arch one, Cranmer, one
Hath crawl'd into the favour of the king,
And is his oracle.

NOR.   He is vex'd at something.

SUR. I would 'twere something that would fret the string,
The master-cord on 's heart!

Enter KING, *reading of a schedule, and* LOVELL.

SUF.   The king, the king!

KING. What piles of wealth hath he accumulated

To his own portion! and what expense by the hour
Seems to flow from him! How, i' the name of thrift,
Does he rake this together? Now, my lords,   110
Saw you the cardinal?

NOR.   My lord, we have
Stood here observing him: some strange commotion
Is in his brain: he bites his lip, and starts;
Stops on a sudden, looks upon the ground,
Then lays his finger on his temple; straight
Springs out into fast gait; then stops again,
Strikes his breast hard, and anon he casts
His eye against the moon: in most strange postures
We have seen him set himself.

KING.   It may well be;
There is a mutiny in 's mind. This morning   120
Papers of state he sent me to peruse,
As I required: and wot you what I found
There, on my conscience, put unwittingly?
Forsooth, an inventory, thus importing,
The several parcels of his plate, his treasure,
Rich stuffs, and ornaments of household, which
I find at such proud rate that it out-speaks
Possession of a subject.

NOR.   It's heaven's will:
Some spirit put this paper in the packet,
To bless your eye withal.

KING.   If we did think   130
His contemplation were above the earth,
And fix'd on spiritual object, he should still
Dwell in his musings: but I am afraid
His thinkings are below the moon, not worth
His serious considering.

          [*King takes his seat; whispers Lovell, who
                    goes to the Cardinal.*

WOL.   Heaven forgive me!
Ever God bless your highness!

KING.   Good my lord,
You are full of heavenly stuff, and bear the inventory
Of your best graces in your mind; the which
You were now running o'er: you have scarce time
To steal from spiritual leisure a brief span   140

To keep your earthly audit: sure, in that
I deem you an ill husband, and am glad
To have you therein my companion.

WOL.   Sir,
For holy offices I have a time; a time
To think upon the part of business which
I bear i' the state; and nature does require
Her times of preservation, which perforce
I, her frail son, amongst my brethren mortal,
Must give my tendance to.

KING.   You have said well.

WOL. And ever may your highness yoke together,   150
As I will lend you cause, my doing well
With my well saying!

KING.   'Tis well said again;
And 'tis a kind of good deed to say well:
And yet words are no deeds. My father loved you:
He said he did, and with his deed did crown
His word upon you. Since I had my office,
I have kept you next my heart; have not alone
Employ'd you where high profits might come home,
But pared my present havings, to bestow
My bounties upon you.

WOL.   *[Aside]* What should this mean?   160

SUR. *[Aside]* The Lord increase this business!

KING.   Have I not made you
The prime man of the state? I pray you, tell me,
If what I now pronounce you have found true:
And, if you may confess it, say withal,
If you are bound to us or no. What say you?

WOL. My sovereign, I confess your royal graces,
Shower'd on me daily, have been more than could
My studied purposes requite; which went
Beyond all man's endeavours: my endeavours
Have ever come too short of my desires,   170
Yet filed with my abilities: mine own ends
Have been mine so that evermore they pointed
To the good of your most sacred person and
The profit of the state. For your great graces
Heap'd upon me, poor undeserver, I
Can nothing render but allegiant thanks,

My prayers to heaven for you, my loyalty,
Which ever has and ever shall be growing,
Till death, that winter, kill it.

  KING.   Fairly answer'd;
A loyal and obedient subject is   180
Therein illustrated: the honour of it
Does pay the act of it; as, i' the contrary,
The foulness is the punishment. I presume
That, as my hand has open'd bounty to you,
My heart dropp'd love, my power rain'd honour, more
On you than any; so your hand and heart,
Your brain and every function of your power,
Should, notwithstanding that your bond of duty,
As 'twere in love's particular, be more
To me, your friend, than any.

  WOL.   I do profess   190
That for your highness' good I ever labour'd
More than mine own; that am, have, and will be—
Though all the world should crack their duty to you,
And throw it from their soul; though perils did
Abound, as thick as thought could make 'em, and
Appear in forms more horrid—yet my duty,
As doth a rock against the chiding flood,
Should the approach of this wild river break,
And stand unshaken yours.

  KING.   'Tis nobly spoken.
Take notice, lords, he has a loyal breast,   200
For you have seen him open 't. [*Giving him papers.*] Read o'er
        this;
And after, this: and then to breakfast with
What appetite you have.

              [*Exit King, frowning upon the Cardinal: the nobles
                  throng after him, smiling and whispering.*

  WOL.   What should this mean?
What sudden anger's this? how have I reap'd it?
He parted frowning from me, as if ruin
Leap'd from his eyes. So looks the chafed lion
Upon the daring huntsman that has gall'd him;
Then makes him nothing. I must read this paper;
I fear, the story of his anger. 'Tis so;
This paper has undone me: 'tis the account   210

Of all that world of wealth I have drawn together
For mine own ends; indeed, to gain the popedom,
And fee my friends in Rome. O negligence!
Fit for a fool to fall by: what cross devil
Made me put this main secret in the packet
I sent the king? Is there no way to cure this?
No new device to beat this from his brains?
I know 'twill stir him strongly; yet I know
A way, if it take right, in spite of fortune
Will bring me off again. What 's this? 'To the Pope!'   220
The letter, as I live, with all the business
I writ to 's holiness. Nay then, farewell!
I have touch'd the highest point of all my greatness;
And, from that full meridian of my glory,
I haste now to my setting: I shall fall
Like a bright exhalation in the evening,
And no man see me more.

Re-enter to WOLSEY *the* DUKES OF NORFOLK *and* SUFFOLK, *the*
EARL OF SURREY, *and the* LORD CHAMBERLAIN.

NOR. Hear the king's pleasure, cardinal: who commands you
To render up the great seal presently
Into our hands; and to confine yourself   230
To Asher-house, my Lord of Winchester's,
Till you hear further from his highness.
WOL.   Stay:
Where's your commission, lords? words cannot carry
Authority so weighty.
SUF.   Who dare cross 'em,
Bearing the king's will from his mouth expressly?
WOL. Till I find more than will or words to do it—
I mean your malice—know, officious lords,
I dare, and must deny it. Now I feel
Of what coarse metal ye are moulded—envy:
How eagerly ye follow my disgraces,   240
As if it fed ye! and how sleek and wanton
Ye appear in every thing may bring my ruin!
Follow your envious courses, men of malice;
You have Christian warrant for 'em, and, no doubt,
In time will find their fit rewards. That seal

You ask with such a violence, the king,
Mine and your master, with his own hand gave me;
Bade me enjoy it, with the place and honours,
During my life; and, to confirm his goodness,
Tied it by letters-patents: now, who 'll take it?   250
 Sur. The king, that gave it.
 Wol.   It must be himself, then.
 Sur. Thou art a proud traitor, priest.
 Wol.   Proud lord, thou liest:
Within these forty hours Surrey durst better
Have burnt that tongue than said so.
 Sur.   Thy ambition,
Thou scarlet sin, robb'd this bewailing land
Of noble Buckingham, my father-in-law:
The heads of all thy brother cardinals,
With thee and all thy best parts bound together,
Weigh'd not a hair of his. Plague of your policy!
You sent me deputy for Ireland;   260
Far from his succour, from the king, from all
That might have mercy on the fault thou gavest him;
Whilst your great goodness, out of holy pity,
Absolved him with an axe.
 Wol.   This, and all else
This talking lord can lay upon my credit,
I answer, is most false. The duke by law
Found his deserts. How innocent I was
From any private malice in his end,
His noble jury and foul cause can witness.
If I loved many words, lord, I should tell you   270
You have as little honesty as honour,
That in the way of loyalty and truth
Toward the king, my ever royal master,
Dare mate a sounder man than Surrey can be,
And all that love his follies.
 Sur.   By my soul,
Your long coat, priest, protects you; thou shouldst feel
My sword i' the life-blood of thee else. My lords,
Can ye endure to hear this arrogance?
And from this fellow? If we live thus tamely,
To be thus jaded by a piece of scarlet,   280
Farewell nobility; let his grace go forward,

And dare us with his cap like larks.

WOL.   All goodness
Is poison to thy stomach.

SUR.   Yes, that goodness
Of gleaning all the land's wealth into one,
Into your own hands, cardinal, by extortion;
The goodness of your intercepted packets
You writ to the pope against the king: your goodness,
Since you provoke me, shall be most notorious.
My Lord of Norfolk, as you are truly noble,
As you respect the common good, the state   290
Of our despised nobility, our issues,
Who, if he live, will scarce be gentlemen,
Produce the grand sum of his sins, the articles
Collected from his life. I 'll startle you
Worse than the sacring bell, when the brown wench
Lay kissing in your arms, lord cardinal.

WOL. How much, methinks, I could despise this man,
But that I am bound in charity against it!

NOR. Those articles, my lord, are in the king's hand;
But, thus much, they are foul ones.

WOL.   So much fairer   310
And spotless shall mine innocence arise,
When the king knows my truth.

SUR.   This cannot save you:
I thank my memory, I yet remember
Some of these articles, and out they shall.
Now, if you can blush and cry 'guilty,' cardinal,
You 'll show a little honesty.

WOL.   Speak on, sir;
I dare your worst objections: if I blush,
It is to see a nobleman want manners.

SUR. I had rather want those than my head. Have at you!
First that, without the king's assent or knowledge,   310
You wrought to be a legate; by which power
You maim'd the jurisdiction of all bishops.

NOR. Then that in all you writ to Rome, or else
To foreign princes, 'Ego et Rex meus'
Was still inscribed; in which you brought the king
To be your servant.

SUF.   Then that, without the knowledge

Either of king or council, when you went
Ambassador to the emperor, you made bold
To carry into Flanders the great seal.

    SUR. Item, you sent a large commission   320
To Gregory de Cassado, to conclude,
Without the king's will or the state's allowance,
A league between his highness and Ferrara.

    SUF. That, out of mere ambition, you have caused
Your holy hat to be stamp'd on the king's coin.

    SUR. Then, that you have sent innumerable substance—
By what means got, I leave to your own conscience—
To furnish Rome, and to prepare the ways
You have for dignities, to the mere undoing
Of all the kingdom. Many more there are;   330
Which, since they are of you and odious,
I will not taint my mouth with.

    CHAM.   O my lord!
Press not a falling man too far; 'tis virtue:
His faults lie open to the laws; let them,
Not you, correct him. My heart weeps to see him
So little of his great self.

    SUR.   I forgive him.

    SUF. Lord cardinal, the king's further pleasure is—
Because all those things you have done of late,
By your power legatine, within this kingdom,
Fall into the compass of a præmunire—   340
That therefore such a writ be sued against you;
To forfeit all your goods, lands, tenements,
Chattels, and whatsoever, and to be
Out of the king's protection. This is my charge.

    NOR. And so we 'll leave you to your meditations
How to live better. For your stubborn answer
About the giving back the great seal to us,
The king shall know it, and, no doubt, shall thank you.
So fare you well, my little good lord cardinal.

                             [*Exeunt all but Wolsey.*

    WOL. So farewell to the little good you bear me.   350
Farewell! a long farewell, to all my greatness!
This is the state of man: to-day he puts forth
The tender leaves of hopes; to-morrow blossoms,
And bears his blushing honours thick upon him;

The third day comes a frost, a killing frost,
And, when he thinks, good easy man, full surely
His greatness is a-ripening, nips his root,
And then he falls, as I do. I have ventured,
Like little wanton boys that swim on bladders,
This many summers in a sea of glory,   360
But far beyond my depth: my high-blown pride
At length broke under me, and now has left me,
Weary and old with service, to the mercy
Of a rude stream that must for ever hide me.
Vain pomp and glory of this world, I hate ye:
I feel my heart new open'd. O, how wretched
Is that poor man that hangs on princes' favours!
There is, betwixt that smile we would aspire to,
That sweet aspect of princes, and their ruin,
More pangs and fears than wars or women have: 370
And when he falls, he falls like Lucifer,
Never to hope again.

Enter CROMWELL, *and stands amazed.*

                            Why, how now, Cromwell!
  CROM. I have no power to speak, sir.
  WOL.   What, amazed
At my misfortunes? can thy spirit wonder
A great man should decline? Nay, an you weep,
I am fall'n indeed.
  CROM.   How does your grace?
  WOL.   Why, well;
Never so truly happy, my good Cromwell.
I know myself now; and I feel within me
A peace above all earthly dignities,
A still and quiet conscience. The king has cured me,   380
I humbly thank his grace; and from these shoulders,
These ruin'd pillars, out of pity, taken
A load would sink a navy, too much honour.
O, 'tis a burden, Cromwell, 'tis a burden
Too heavy for a man that hopes for heaven!
  CROM. I am glad your grace has made that right use of it.
  WOL. I hope I have: I am able now, methinks,
Out of a fortitude of soul I feel,

To endure more miseries and greater far
Than my weak-hearted enemies dare offer.   390
What news abroad?

CROM.   The heaviest and the worst
Is your displeasure with the king.

WOL.   God bless him!

CROM. The next is, that Sir Thomas More is chosen
Lord chancellor in your place.

WOL.   That 's somewhat sudden:
But he 's a learned man. May he continue
Long in his highness' favour, and do justice
For truth's sake and his conscience; that his bones,
When he has run his course and sleeps in blessings,
May have a tomb of orphans' tears wept on 'em!
What more?

CROM. That Cranmer is return'd with welcome,   400
Install'd lord archbishop of Canterbury.

WOL. That 's news indeed.

CROM.   Last, that the Lady Anne,
Whom the king hath in secrecy long married,
This day was view'd in open as his queen,
Going to chapel; and the voice is now
Only about her coronation.

WOL. There was the weight that pull'd me down. O Cromwell,
The king has gone beyond me: all my glories
In that one woman I have lost for ever:
No sun shall ever usher forth mine honours,   410
Or gild again the noble troops that waited
Upon my smiles. Go, get thee from me, Cromwell;
I am a poor fall'n man, unworthy now
To be thy lord and master: seek the king;
That sun, I pray, may never set! I have told him
What and how true thou art: he will advance thee;
Some little memory of me will stir him—
I know his noble nature—not to let
Thy hopeful service perish too: good Cromwell,
Neglect him not; make use now, and provide   420
For thine own future safety.

CROM.   O my lord,
Must I then leave you? must I needs forgo
So good, so noble and so true a master?

Bear witness, all that have not hearts of iron,
With what a sorrow Cromwell leaves his lord.
The king shall have my service, but my prayers
For ever and for ever shall be yours.

WOL. Cromwell, I did not think to shed a tear
In all my miseries; but thou hast forced me,
Out of thy honest truth, to play the woman.   430
Let's dry our eyes: and thus far hear me, Cromwell;
And, when I am forgotten, as I shall be,
And sleep in dull cold marble, where no mention
Of me more must be heard of, say, I taught thee;
Say, Wolsey, that once trod the ways of glory,
And sounded all the depths and shoals of honour,
Found thee a way, out of his wreck, to rise in;
A sure and safe one, though thy master miss'd it.
Mark but my fall and that that ruin'd me.
Cromwell, I charge thee, fling away ambition: 440
By that sin fell the angels; how can man then,
The image of his Maker, hope to win by it?
Love thyself last: cherish those hearts that hate thee;
Corruption wins not more than honesty.
Still in thy right hand carry gentle peace,
To silence envious tongues. Be just, and fear not:
Let all the ends thou aim'st at be thy country's,
Thy God's, and truth's; then if thou fall'st, O Cromwell,
Thou fall'st a blessed martyr! Serve the king;
And prithee, lead me in: 450
There take an inventory of all I have,
To the last penny; 'tis the king's: my robe,
And my integrity to heaven, is all
I dare now call mine own. O Cromwell, Cromwell!
Had I but served my God with half the zeal
I served my king, he would not in mine age
Have left me naked to mine enemies.

CROM. Good sir, have patience.

WOL.   So I have. Farewell
The hopes of court! my hopes in heaven do dwell.

                                                    [*Exeunt.*

ACT IV.

Scene I. *A Street in Westminster.*

Enter two Gentlemen, *meeting one another.*

First Gent. You're well met once again.

Sec. Gent.   So are you.

First Gent. You come to take your stand here and behold
The Lady Anne pass from her coronation?

Sec. Gent. 'Tis all my business. At our last encounter,
The Duke of Buckingham came from his trial.

First Gent. 'Tis very true: but that time offer'd sorrow;
This, general joy.

Sec. Gent.   'Tis well: the citizens,
I am sure, have shown at full their royal minds—
As, let 'em have their rights, they are ever forward—
In celebration of this day with shows,   10
Pageants and sights of honour.

First Gent.   Never greater,
Nor, I 'll assure you, better taken, sir.

Sec. Gent. May I be bold to ask what that contains,
That paper in your hand?

First Gent.   Yes; 'tis the list
Of those that claim their offices this day
By custom of the coronation.
The Duke of Suffolk is the first, and claims
To be high-steward; next, the Duke of Norfolk,
He to be earl marshal: you may read the rest.

Sec. Gent. I thank you, sir: had I not known those customs, 20
I should have been beholding to your paper.
But, I beseech you, what 's become of Katharine,
The princess dowager? how goes her business?

First Gent. That I can tell you too. The Archbishop
Of Canterbury, accompanied with other
Learned and reverend fathers of his order,
Held a late court at Dunstable, six miles off
From Ampthill, where the princess lay; to which
She was often cited by them, but appear'd not:
And, to be short, for not appearance and   30
The king's late scruple, by the main assent

63

Of all these learned men she was divorced,
And the late marriage made of none effect:
Since which she was removed to Kimbolton,
Where she remains now sick.

 SEC. GENT.   Alas, good lady!

                 [*Trumpets.*

The trumpets sound: stand close, the queen is coming.

                 [*Hautboys.*

THE ORDER OF THE CORONATION.

1. *A lively Flourish of Trumpets.*
2. *Then two* Judges.
3. LORD CHANCELLOR, *with purse and mace before him.*
4. Choristers, *singing.*   Musicians.
5. Mayor of London, *bearing the mace. Then* Garter, *in his coat of arms, and on his head he wears a gilt copper crown.*
6. MARQUESS DORSET, *bearing a sceptre of gold, on his head a demi-coronal of gold. With him, the* EARL OF SURREY, *bearing the rod of silver with the dove, crowned with an earl's coronet. Collars of SS.*
7. DUKE OF SUFFOLK, *in his robe of estate, his coronet on his head, bearing a long white wand, as high-steward. With him, the* DUKE OF NORFOLK, *with the rod of marshalship, a coronet on his head. Collars of SS.*
8. *A canopy borne by four of the* Cinque-ports; *under it, the* QUEEN *in her robe; in her hair richly adorned with pearl, crowned. On each side her, the* BISHOPS OF LONDON *and* WINCHESTER.
9. *The old* DUCHESS OF NORFOLK, *in a coronal of gold, wrought with flowers, bearing the* QUEEN's *train.*
10. *Certain* Ladies *or* Countesses, *with plain circlets of gold without flowers.*
  They pass over the stage in order and state.

 SEC. GENT. A royal train, believe me. These I know:
Who 's that that bears the sceptre?

 FIRST GENT.   Marquess Dorset:
And that the Earl of Surrey, with the rod.

 SEC. GENT. A bold brave gentleman. That should be   40
The Duke of Suffolk?

FIRST GENT.   'Tis the same: high-steward.

SEC. GENT. And that my Lord of Norfolk?

FIRST GENT.   Yes.

SEC. GENT.   [*Looking on the Queen*] Heaven bless thee!
Thou hast the sweetest face I ever look'd on.
Sir, as I have a soul, she is an angel;
Our king has all the Indies in his arms,
And more and richer, when he strains that lady:
I cannot blame his conscience.

FIRST GENT.   They that bear
The cloth of honour over her, are four barons
Of the Cinque-ports.

SEC. GENT. Those men are happy; and so are all are near her. 50
I take it, she that carries up the train
Is that old noble lady, Duchess of Norfolk.

FIRST GENT. It is; and all the rest are countesses.

SEC. GENT. Their coronets say so. These are stars indeed,
And sometimes falling ones.

FIRST GENT.   No more of that.

> [*Exit procession; and then a
> great flourish of trumpets.*

Enter a third Gentleman.

God save you, sir! where have you been broiling?

THIRD GENT. Among the crowd i' the abbey; where a finger
Could not be wedged in more: I am stifled
With the mere rankness of their joy.

SEC. GENT.   You saw
The ceremony?

THIRD GENT. That I did.

FIRST GENT.   How was it?   60

THIRD GENT. Well worth the seeing.

SEC. GENT.   Good sir, speak it to us.

THIRD GENT. As well as I am able. The rich stream
Of lords and ladies, having brought the queen
To a prepared place in the choir, fell off
A distance from her; while her grace sat down
To rest awhile, some half an hour or so,
In a rich chair of state, opposing freely
The beauty of her person to the people.

Believe me, sir, she is the goodliest woman
That ever lay by man: which when the people   70
Had the full view of, such a noise arose
As the shrouds make at sea in a stiff tempest,
As loud and to as many tunes: hats, cloaks,—
Doublets, I think,—flew up; and had their faces
Been loose, this day they had been lost. Such joy
I never saw before. Great-bellied women,
That had not half a week to go, like rams
In the old time of war, would shake the press,
And make 'em reel before 'em. No man living
Could say 'This is my wife' there, all were woven   80
So strangely in one piece.

    SEC. GENT.   But what follow'd?

    THIRD GENT. At length her grace rose, and with modest paces
Came to the altar, where she kneel'd and saintlike
Cast her fair eyes to heaven and pray'd devoutly;
Then rose again and bow'd her to the people;
When by the Archbishop of Canterbury
She had all the royal makings of a queen,
As holy oil, Edward Confessor's crown,
The rod, and bird of peace, and all such emblems
Laid nobly on her: which perform'd, the choir,   90
With all the choicest music of the kingdom,
Together sung 'Te Deum.' So she parted,
And with the same full state paced back again
To York-place, where the feast is held.

    FIRST GENT.   Sir,
You must no more call it York-place; that's past;
For, since the cardinal fell, that title's lost:
'Tis now the king's, and call'd Whitehall.

    THIRD GENT.   I know it;
But 'tis so lately alter'd, that the old name
Is fresh about me.

    SEC. GENT.   What two reverend bishops
Were those that went on each side of the queen?   100

    THIRD GENT. Stokesly and Gardiner; the one of Winchester,
Newly preferr'd from the king's secretary,
The other, London.

    SEC. GENT.   He of Winchester
Is held no great good lover of the archbishop's,

The virtuous Cranmer.

    THIRD GENT.   All the land knows that:

However, yet there is no great breach; when it comes,

Cranmer will find a friend will not shrink from him.

    SEC. GENT. Who may that be, I pray you?

    THIRD GENT.   Thomas Cromwell;

A man in much esteem with the king, and truly

A worthy friend. The king has made him master   110

O' the jewel house,

And one, already, of the privy council.

    SEC. GENT. He will deserve more.

    THIRD GENT.   Yes, without all doubt.

Come, gentlemen, ye shall go my way,

Which is to the court, and there ye shall be my guests:

Something I can command. As I walk thither,

I 'll tell ye more.

    BOTH.   You may command us, sir.   [*Exeunt.*

SCENE II. *Kimbolton.*

Enter KATHARINE, *Dowager, sick; led between* GRIFFITH, *her
Gentleman Usher, and* PATIENCE, *her woman.*

    GRIF. How does your grace?

    KATH.   O Griffith, sick to death!

My legs, like loaden branches, bow to the earth,

Willing to leave their burthen. Reach a chair.

So; now, methinks, I feel a little ease.

Didst thou not tell me, Griffith, as thou led'st me,

That the great child of honour, Cardinal Wolsey,

Was dead?

    GRIF. Yes, madam; but I think your grace,

Out of the pain you suffer'd, gave no ear to 't.

    KATH. Prithee, good Griffith, tell me how he died:

If well, he stepp'd before me, happily,   10

For my example.

    GRIF.   Well, the voice goes, madam:

For after the stout Earl Northumberland

Arrested him at York, and brought him forward,

As a man sorely tainted, to his answer,
He fell sick suddenly, and grew so ill
He could not sit his mule.

   KATH.   Alas, poor man!

   GRIF. At last, with easy roads, he came to Leicester,
Lodged in the abbey; where the reverend abbot,
With all his covent, honourably received him;
To whom he gave these words, 'O father abbot,   20
An old man, broken with the storms of state,
Is come to lay his weary bones among ye;
Give him a little earth for charity!'
So went to bed; where eagerly his sickness
Pursued him still; and three nights after this,
About the hour of eight, which he himself
Foretold should be his last, full of repentance,
Continual meditations, tears and sorrows,
He gave his honours to the world again,
His blessed part to heaven, and slept in peace.   30

   KATH. So may he rest; his faults lie gently on him!
Yet thus far, Griffith, give me leave to speak him,
And yet with charity. He was a man
Of an unbounded stomach, ever ranking
Himself with princes; one that by suggestion
Tied all the kingdom: simony was fair-play:
His own opinion was his law: i' the presence
He would say untruths, and be ever double
Both in his words and meaning: he was never,
But where he meant to ruin, pitiful: 40
His promises were, as he then was, mighty;
But his performance, as he is now, nothing:
Of his own body he was ill, and gave
The clergy ill example.

   GRIF.   Noble madam,
Men's evil manners live in brass; their virtues
We write in water. May it please your highness
To hear me speak his good now?

   KATH.   Yes, good Griffith;
I were malicious else.

   GRIF.   This cardinal,
Though from an humble stock, undoubtedly
Was fashion'd to much honour from his cradle.   50

He was a scholar, and a ripe and good one;
Exceeding wise, fair-spoken and persuading:
Lofty and sour to them that loved him not,
But to those men that sought him, sweet as summer.
And though he were unsatisfied in getting,
Which was a sin, yet in bestowing, madam,
He was most princely: ever witness for him
Those twins of learning that he raised in you,
Ipswich and Oxford! one of which fell with him,
Unwilling to outlive the good that did it;   60
The other, though unfinish'd, yet so famous,
So excellent in art and still so rising,
That Christendom shall ever speak his virtue.
His overthrow heap'd happiness upon him;
For then, and not till then, he felt himself,
And found the blessedness of being little:
And, to add greater honours to his age
Than man could give him, he died fearing God.
    KATH. After my death I wish no other herald,
No other speaker of my living actions,   70
To keep mine honour from corruption,
But such an honest chronicler as Griffith.
Whom I most hated living, thou hast made me,
With thy religious truth and modesty,
Now in his ashes honour: peace be with him!
Patience, be near me still; and set me lower:
I have not long to trouble thee. Good Griffith,
Cause the musicians play me that sad note
I named my knell, whilst I sit meditating
On that celestial harmony I go to.   80
                                  [*Sad and solemn music.*

   GRIF. She is asleep: good wench, let 's sit down quiet,
For fear we wake her: softly, gentle Patience.

The vision. Enter, solemnly tripping one after another, six personages,
  clad in white robes, wearing on their heads garlands of bays, and
  golden vizards on their faces; branches of bays or palm in their hands.
  They first congee unto her, then dance; and, at certain changes, the
  first two hold a spare garland over her head; at which the other four
  make reverent curtsies; then the two that held the garland deliver the
  same to the other next two, who observe the same order in their

changes, and holding the garland over her head: which done, they deliver the same garland to the last two, who likewise observe the same order: at which, as it were by inspiration, she makes in her sleep signs of rejoicing, and holdeth up her hands to heaven: and so in their dancing vanish, carrying the garland with them. The music continues.

KATH. Spirits of peace, where are ye? are ye all gone,
And leave me here in wretchedness behind ye?
   GRIF. Madam, we are here.
   KATH.   It is not you I call for:
Saw ye none enter since I slept?
   GRIF.   None, madam.
   KATH. No? Saw you not even now a blessed troop
Invite me to a banquet, whose bright faces
Cast thousand beams upon me, like the sun?
They promised me eternal happiness,   90
And brought me garlands, Griffith, which I feel
I am not worthy yet to wear: I shall, assuredly.
   GRIF. I am most joyful, madam, such good dreams
Possess your fancy.
   KATH.   Bid the music leave;
They are harsh and heavy to me.   [*Music ceases.*
   PAT.   Do you note
How much her grace is alter'd on the sudden?
How long her face is drawn! how pale she looks,
And of an earthy cold! Mark her eyes!
   GRIF. She is going, wench: pray, pray.
   PAT.   Heaven comfort her!

Enter a Messenger.

   MESS. An 't like your grace,—
   KATH.   You are a saucy fellow: 100
Deserve we no more reverence?
   GRIF.   You are to blame,
Knowing she will not lose her wonted greatness,
To use so rude behaviour: go to, kneel.
   MESS. I humbly do entreat your highness' pardon;
My haste made me unmannerly. There is staying
A gentleman, sent from the king, to see you.

KATH. Admit him entrance, Griffith: but this fellow
Let me ne'er see again.   [*Exeunt Griffith and Messenger.*

Re-enter GRIFFITH, *with* CAPUCIUS.

                    If my sight fail not,
You should be lord ambassador from the emperor,
My royal nephew, and your name Capucius.   110
    CAP. Madam, the same; your servant.
    KATH.   O, my lord,
The times and titles now are alter'd strangely
With me since first you knew me. But, I pray you,
What is your pleasure with me?
    CAP.   Noble lady,
First, mine own service to your grace; the next,
The king's request that I would visit you;
Who grieves much for your weakness, and by me
Sends you his princely commendations,
And heartily entreats you take good comfort.
    KATH. O my good lord, that comfort comes too late;   120
'Tis like a pardon after execution:
That gentle physic, given in time, had cured me;
But now I am past all comforts here but prayers.
How does his highness?
    CAP.   Madam, in good health.
    KATH. So may he ever do! and ever flourish,
When I shall dwell with worms, and my poor name
Banish'd the kingdom! Patience, is that letter,
I caused you write, yet sent away?
    PAT.   No, madam.
                        [*Giving it to Katharine.*
    KATH. Sir, I most humbly pray you to deliver
This to my lord the king.
    CAP.   Most willing, madam.   130
    KATH. In which I have commended to his goodness
The model of our chaste loves, his young daughter,—
The dews of heaven fall thick in blessings on her!—
Beseeching him to give her virtuous breeding—
She is young and of a noble modest nature:
I hope she will deserve well—and a little
To love her for her mother's sake, that loved him,

Heaven knows how dearly. My next poor petition
Is that his noble grace would have some pity
Upon my wretched women, that so long   140
Have follow'd both my fortunes faithfully:
Of which there is not one, I dare avow,—
And now I should not lie—but will deserve,
For virtue and true beauty of the soul,
For honesty and decent carriage,
A right good husband, let him be a noble:
And, sure, those men are happy that shall have 'em.
The last is, for my men; they are the poorest,
But poverty could never draw 'em from me;
That they may have their wages duly paid 'em,   150
And something over to remember me by:
If heaven had pleased to have given me longer life
And able means, we had not parted thus.
These are the whole contents: and, good my lord,
By that you love the dearest in this world,
As you wish Christian peace to souls departed,
Stand these poor people's friend, and urge the king
To do me this last right.

CAP.   By heaven, I will,
Or let me lose the fashion of a man!

KATH. I thank you, honest lord. Remember me   160
In all humility unto his highness:
Say his long trouble now is passing
Out of this world; tell him, in death I bless'd him,
For so I will. Mine eyes grow dim. Farewell,
My lord. Griffith, farewell. Nay, Patience,
You must not leave me yet: I must to bed;
Call in more women. When I am dead, good wench,
Let me be used with honour: strew me over
With maiden flowers, that all the world may know
I was a chaste wife to my grave: embalm me,   170
Then lay me forth; although unqueen'd, yet like
A queen, and daughter to a king, inter me.
I can no more.   [*Exeunt, leading Katharine.*

ACT V.

SCENE I. *London. A Gallery in the Palace.*

Enter GARDINER, Bishop of Winchester, *a Page with a torch before him, met by* SIR THOMAS LOVELL.

GAR. It 's one o'clock, boy, is't not?

BOY.   It hath struck.

GAR. These should be hours for necessities,
Not for delights; times to repair our nature
With comforting repose, and not for us
To waste these times. Good hour of night, Sir Thomas!
Whither so late?

LOV.   Came you from the king, my lord?

GAR. I did, Sir Thomas, and left him at primero
With the Duke of Suffolk.

LOV.   I must to him too,
Before he go to bed. I 'll take my leave.

GAR. Not yet, Sir Thomas Lovell. What 's the matter?   10
It seems you are in haste: an if there be
No great offence belongs to 't, give your friend
Some touch of your late business: affairs that walk,
As they say spirits do, at midnight, have
In them a wilder nature than the business
That seeks dispatch by day.

LOV.   My lord, I love you;
And durst commend a secret to your ear
Much weightier than this work. The queen's in labour,
They say, in great extremity; and fear'd
She 'll with the labour end.

GAR.   The fruit she goes with   20
I pray for heartily, that it may find
Good time, and live: but for the stock, Sir Thomas,
I wish it grubb'd up now.

LOV.   Methinks I could
Cry the amen; and yet my conscience says
She's a good creature, and, sweet lady, does
Deserve our better wishes.

GAR.   But, sir, sir,

Hear me, Sir Thomas: you're a gentleman
Of mine own way; I know you wise, religious;
And, let me tell you, it will ne'er be well,
'Twill not, Sir Thomas Lovell, take 't of me,   30
Till Cranmer, Cromwell, her two hands, and she,
Sleep in their graves.

    Lov.   Now, sir, you speak of two
The most remark'd i' the kingdom. As for Cromwell,
Beside that of the jewel house, is made master
O' the rolls, and the king's secretary; further, sir,
Stands in the gap and trade of moe preferments,
With which the time will load him. The archbishop
Is the king's hand and tongue; and who dare speak
One syllable against him?

    Gar.   Yes, yes, Sir Thomas,
There are that dare; and I myself have ventured   40
To speak my mind of him: and indeed this day,
Sir, I may tell it you, I think I have
Incensed the lords o' the council that he is—
For so I know he is, they know he is—
A most arch-heretic, a pestilence
That does infect the land: with which they moved
Have broken with the king; who hath so far
Given ear to our complaint, of his great grace
And princely care foreseeing those fell mischiefs
Our reasons laid before him, hath commanded   50
To-morrow morning to the council-board
He be convented. He's a rank weed, Sir Thomas,
And we must root him out. From your affairs
I hinder you too long: good night, Sir Thomas.

    Lov. Many good nights, my lord: I rest your servant.

                         [Exeunt Gardiner and Page.

Enter King *and* Suffolk.

    King. Charles, I will play no more to-night;
My mind's not on 't; you are too hard for me.
    Suf. Sir, I did never win of you before.
    King. But little, Charles,
Nor shall not, when my fancy's on my play.   60
Now, Lovell, from the queen what is the news?

Lov. I could not personally deliver to her
What you commanded me, but by her woman
I sent your message; who return'd her thanks
In the great'st humbleness, and desired your highness
Most heartily to pray for her.
King.   What say'st thou, ha?
To pray for her? what, is she crying out?
Lov. So said her woman, and that her sufferance made
Almost each pang a death.
King.   Alas, good lady!
Suf. God safely quit her of her burthen, and   70
With gentle travail, to the gladding of
Your highness with an heir!
King.   'Tis midnight, Charles;
Prithee, to bed; and in thy prayers remember
The estate of my poor queen. Leave me alone;
For I must think of that which company
Would not be friendly to.
Suf.   I wish your highness
A quiet night, and my good mistress will
Remember in my prayers.
King.   Charles, good night.   [*Exit Suffolk.*

Enter Sir Anthony Denny.

Well, sir, what follows?
Den. Sir, I have brought my lord the archbishop,   80
As you commanded me.
King.   Ha! Canterbury?
Den. Ay, my good lord.
King.   'Tis true: where is he, Denny?
Den. He attends your highness' pleasure.
King.   Bring him to us.
                                                [*Exit Denny.*
Lov. [*Aside*] This is about that which the bishop spake:
I am happily come hither.

Re-enter Denny, *with* Cranmer.

King. Avoid the gallery. [*Lovell seems to stay.*] Ha! I have said.
      Be gone.

What!   [*Exeunt Lovell and Denny.*

 CRAN. [*Aside*] I am fearful: wherefore frowns he thus?
'Tis his aspect of terror. All 's not well.

 KING. How now, my lord! you do desire to know
Wherefore I sent for you.

 CRAN. [*Kneeling*] It is my duty   90
To attend your highness' pleasure.

 KING.   Pray you, arise,
My good and gracious Lord of Canterbury.
Come, you and I must walk a turn together;
I have news to tell you: come, come, give me your hand.
Ah, my good lord, I grieve at what I speak,
And am right sorry to repeat what follows:
I have, and most unwillingly, of late
Heard many grievous, I do say, my lord,
Grievous complaints of you; which, being consider'd,
Have moved us and our council, that you shall   100
This morning come before us; where, I know,
You cannot with such freedom purge yourself,
But that, till further trial in those charges
Which will require your answer, you must take
Your patience to you and be well contented
To make your house our Tower: you a brother of us,
It fits we thus proceed, or else no witness
Would come against you.

 CRAN. [*Kneeling*] I humbly thank your highness;
And am right glad to catch this good occasion
Most throughly to be winnow'd, where my chaff   110
And corn shall fly asunder: for, I know,
There's none stands under more calumnious tongues
Than I myself, poor man.

 KING.   Stand up, good Canterbury:
Thy truth and thy integrity is rooted
In us, thy friend: give me thy hand, stand up:
Prithee, let's walk. Now, by my holidame,
What manner of man are you? My lord, I look'd
You would have given me your petition, that
I should have ta'en some pains to bring together
Yourself and your accusers, and to have heard you,   120
Without indurance further.

CRAN.   Most dread liege,
The good I stand on is my truth and honesty:
If they shall fail, I, with mine enemies,
Will triumph o'er my person; which I weigh not,
Being of those virtues vacant. I fear nothing
What can be said against me.
    KING.   Know you not
How your state stands i' the world, with the whole world?
Your enemies are many, and not small; their practices
Must bear the same proportion; and not ever
The justice and the truth o' the question carries   130
The due o' the verdict with it: at what ease
Might corrupt minds procure knaves as corrupt
To swear against you? Such things have been done.
You are potently opposed, and with a malice
Of as great size. Ween you of better luck,
I mean, in perjured witness, than your master,
Whose minister you are, whiles here he lived
Upon this naughty earth? Go to, go to;
You take a precipice for no leap of danger,
And woo your own destruction.
    CRAN.   God and your majesty   140
Protect mine innocence, or I fall into
The trap is laid for me!
    KING.   Be of good cheer;
They shall no more prevail than we give way to.
Keep comfort to you; and this morning see
You do appear before them. If they shall chance,
In charging you with matters, to commit you,
The best persuasions to the contrary
Fail not to use, and with what vehemency
The occasion shall instruct you: if entreaties
Will render you no remedy, this ring   150
Deliver them, and your appeal to us
There make before them. Look, the good man weeps!
He 's honest, on mine honour. God's blest mother!
I swear he is true-hearted, and a soul
None better in my kingdom. Get you gone,
And do as I have bid you. [*Exit Cranmer.*] He has strangled
His language in his tears.

Enter Old Lady; LOVELL *following.*

GENT.   [*Within*] Come back: what mean you?
OLD L. I 'll not come back; the tidings that I bring
Will make my boldness manners. Now, good angels
Fly o'er thy royal head, and shade thy person   160
Under their blessed wings!
KING.   Now, by thy looks
I guess thy message. Is the queen deliver'd?
Say, ay, and of a boy.
OLD L.   Ay, ay, my liege;
And of a lovely boy: the God of heaven
Both now and ever bless her! 'tis a girl,
Promises boys hereafter. Sir, your queen
Desires your visitation, and to be
Acquainted with this stranger: 'tis as like you
As cherry is to cherry.
KING.   Lovell!
LOV.   Sir?
KING. Give her an hundred marks. I 'll to the queen.   170
                                                      [*Exit.*

OLD L. An hundred marks! By this light, I 'll ha' more.
An ordinary groom is for such payment.
I will have more, or scold it out of him.
Said I for this, the girl was like to him?
I will have more, or else unsay 't; and now,
While it is hot, I 'll put it to the issue.   [*Exeunt.*

SCENE II. *Before the Council-Chamber.*

Pursuivants, Pages, *&c. attending.*

Enter CRANMER, Archbishop of Canterbury.

CRAN. I hope I am not too late; and yet the gentleman
That was sent to me from the council pray'd me
To make great haste. All fast? what means this? Ho!
Who waits there? Sure, you know me?

Enter Keeper.

KEEP.   Yes, my lord;
But yet I cannot help you.
   CRAN. Why?

Enter DOCTOR BUTTS.

   KEEP. Your grace must wait till you be call'd for.
   CRAN.   So.
   BUTTS. [*Aside*] This is a piece of malice. I am glad
I came this way so happily: the king
Shall understand it presently.   [*Exit.*
   CRAN.   [*Aside*] 'Tis Butts,   10
The king's physician: as he pass'd along,
How earnestly he cast his eyes upon me!
Pray heaven, he sound not my disgrace! For certain,
This is of purpose laid by some that hate me—
God turn their hearts! I never sought their malice—
To quench mine honour: they would shame to make me
Wait else at door, a fellow-councillor,
'Mong boys, grooms and lackeys. But their pleasures
Must be fulfill'd, and I attend with patience.

Enter the KING *and* BUTTS *at a window above.*

   BUTTS. I'll show your grace the strangest sight—
   KING.   What's that, Butts?   20
   BUTTS. I think your highness saw this many a day.
   KING. Body o' me, where is it?
   BUTTS.   There, my lord:
The high promotion of his grace of Canterbury;
Who holds his state at door, 'mongst pursuivants,
Pages and footboys.
   KING.   Ha! 'tis he, indeed:
Is this the honour they do one another?
'Tis well there 's one above 'em yet. I had thought
They had parted so much honesty among 'em,
At least good manners, as not thus to suffer
A man of his place and so near our favour   30
To dance attendance on their lordships' pleasures,

And at the door too, like a post with packets.
By holy Mary, Butts, there's knavery:
Let 'em alone, and draw the curtain close;
We shall hear more anon.   [*Exeunt.*

SCENE III. *The Council-Chamber.*

Enter LORD CHANCELLOR, *places himself at the upper end of the table
on the left hand; a seat being left void above him, as for* CANTERBURY'S
seat; DUKE OF SUFFOLK, DUKE OF NORFOLK, SURREY, LORD
CHAMBERLAIN, GARDINER, *seat themselves in order on each side.*
CROMWELL *at lower end, as secretary. Keeper at the door.*

CHAN. Speak to the business, master secretary:
Why are we met in council?
  CROM.   Please your honours,
The chief cause concerns his grace of Canterbury.
  GAR. Has he had knowledge of it?
  CROM.   Yes.
  NOR.   Who waits there?
  KEEP. Without, my noble lords?
  GAR.   Yes.
  KEEP.   My lord archbishop;
And has done half an hour, to know your pleasures.
  CHAN. Let him come in.
  KEEP.   Your grace may enter now.
     [*Cranmer enters and approaches the council-table.*
  CHAN. My good lord archbishop, I 'm very sorry
To sit here at this present and behold
That chair stand empty: but we all are men,   10
In our own natures frail and capable
Of our flesh; few are angels: out of which frailty
And want of wisdom, you, that best should teach us,
Have misdemean'd yourself, and not a little,
Toward the king first, then his laws, in filling
The whole realm, by your teaching and your chaplains,—
For so we are inform'd,—with new opinions,
Divers and dangerous; which are heresies,
And, not reform'd, may prove pernicious.

GAR. Which reformation must be sudden too,   20
My noble lords; for those that tame wild horses
Pace 'em not in their hands to make 'em gentle,
But stop their mouths with stubborn bits and spur 'em,
Till they obey the manage. If we suffer,
Out of our easiness and childish pity
To one man's honour, this contagious sickness,
Farewell all physic: and what follows then?
Commotions, uproars, with a general taint
Of the whole state: as of late days our neighbours,
The upper Germany, can dearly witness,   30
Yet freshly pitied in our memories.

     CRAN. My good lords, hitherto, in all the progress
Both of my life and office, I have labour'd,
And with no little study, that my teaching
And the strong course of my authority
Might go one way, and safely; and the end
Was ever to do well: nor is there living,
I speak it with a single heart, my lords,
A man that more detests, more stirs against,
Both in his private conscience and his place,   40
Defacers of a public peace, than I do.
Pray heaven, the king may never find a heart
With less allegiance in it! Men that make
Envy and crooked malice nourishment
Dare bite the best. I do beseech your lordships,
That, in this case of justice, my accusers,
Be what they will, may stand forth face to face,
And freely urge against me.

SUF.   Nay, my lord,
That cannot be: you are a councillor,
And, by that virtue, no man dare accuse you.   50

     GAR. My lord, because we have business of more moment,
We will be short with you. 'Tis his highness' pleasure,
And our consent, for better trial of you,
From hence you be committed to the Tower;
Where, being but a private man again,
You shall know many dare accuse you boldly,
More than, I fear, you are provided for.

     CRAN. Ah, my good Lord of Winchester, I thank you;
You are always my good friend; if your will pass,

I shall both find your lordship judge and juror,   60
You are so merciful. I see your end;
'Tis my undoing. Love and meekness, lord,
Become a churchman better than ambition:
Win straying souls with modesty again,
Cast none away. That I shall clear myself,
Lay all the weight ye can upon my patience,
I make as little doubt as you do conscience
In doing daily wrongs. I could say more,
But reverence to your calling makes me modest.

    GAR. My lord, my lord, you are a sectary;   70
That's the plain truth: your painted gloss discovers,
To men that understand you, words and weakness.

    CROM. My Lord of Winchester, you are a little,
By your good favour, too sharp; men so noble,
However faulty, yet should find respect
For what they have been: 'tis a cruelty
To load a falling man.

    GAR.   Good master secretary,
I cry your honour mercy; you may, worst
Of all this table, say so.

    CROM.   Why, my lord?

    GAR. Do not I know you for a favourer   80
Of this new sect? ye are not sound.

    CROM.   Not sound?

    GAR. Not sound, I say.

    CROM.   Would you were half so honest!
Men's prayers then would seek you, not their fears.

    GAR. I shall remember this bold language.

    CROM.   Do.
Remember your bold life too.

    CHAN.   This is too much;
Forbear, for shame, my lords.

    GAR.   I have done.

    CROM.   And I.

    CHAN. Then thus for you, my lord: it stands agreed,
I take it, by all voices, that forthwith
You be convey'd to the Tower a prisoner;
There to remain till the king's further pleasure   90
Be known unto us: are you all agreed, lords?

    ALL. We are.

CRAN.   Is there no other way of mercy,
But I must needs to the Tower, my lords?
    GAR.   What other
Would you expect? you are strangely troublesome.
Let some o' the guard be ready there.

Enter Guard.

CRAN.   For me?
Must I go like a traitor thither?
    GAR.   Receive him,
And see him safe i' the Tower.
    CRAN.   Stay, good my lords,
I have a little yet to say. Look there, my lords;
By virtue of that ring, I take my cause
Out of the gripes of cruel men, and give it   100
To a most noble judge, the king my master.
    CHAM. This is the king's ring.
    SUR.   'Tis no counterfeit.
    SUF. 'Tis the right ring, by heaven: I told ye all,
When we first put this dangerous stone a-rolling,
'Twould fall upon ourselves.
    NOR.   Do you think, my lords,
The king will suffer but the little finger
Of this man to be vex'd?
    CHAM.   'Tis now too certain:
How much more is his life in value with him?
Would I were fairly out on 't!
    CROM.   My mind gave me,
In seeking tales and informations   110
Against this man, whose honesty the devil
And his disciples only envy at,
Ye blew the fire that burns ye: now have at ye!

Enter KING, *frowning on them; takes his seat.*

    GAR. Dread sovereign, how much are we bound to heaven
In daily thanks, that gave us such a prince,
Not only good and wise, but most religious:
One that, in all obedience, makes the church
The chief aim of his honour; and, to strengthen

That holy duty, out of dear respect,
His royal self in judgement comes to hear   120
The cause betwixt her and this great offender.

   KING. You were ever good at sudden commendations,
Bishop of Winchester. But know, I come not
To hear such flattery now, and in my presence
They are too thin and bare to hide offences.
To me you cannot reach you play the spaniel,
And think with wagging of your tongue to win me;
But, whatsoe'er thou takest me for, I'm sure
Thou hast a cruel nature and a bloody.
[*To Cranmer*] Good man, sit down. Now let me see the proudest 130
He, that dares most, but wag his finger at thee:
By all that 's holy, he had better starve
Than but once think this place becomes thee not.

   SUR. May it please your grace,—

   KING.   No, sir, it does not please me.
I had thought I had had men of some understanding
And wisdom of my council; but I find none.
Was it discretion, lords, to let this man,
This good man,—few of you deserve that title,—
This honest man, wait like a lousy footboy
At chamber-door? and one as great as you are?   140
Why, what a shame was this! Did my commission
Bid ye so far forget yourselves? I gave ye
Power as he was a councillor to try him,
Not as a groom: there 's some of ye, I see,
More out of malice than integrity,
Would try him to the utmost, had ye mean;
Which ye shall never have while I live.

   CHAN.   Thus far,
My most dread sovereign, may it like your grace
To let my tongue excuse all. What was purposed
Concerning his imprisonment, was rather,   150
If there be faith in men, meant for his trial
And fair purgation to the world, than malice,
I 'm sure, in me.

   KING.   Well, well, my lords, respect him;
Take him and use him well; he's worthy of it.
I will say thus much for him, if a prince
May be beholding to a subject, I

Am, for his love and service, so to him.
Make me no more ado, but all embrace him:
Be friends, for shame, my lords! My Lord of Canterbury,
I have a suit which you must not deny me;   160
That is, a fair young maid that yet wants baptism;
You must be godfather, and answer for her.

    CRAN. The greatest monarch now alive may glory
In such an honour: how may I deserve it,
That am a poor and humble subject to you?

    KING. Come, come, my lord, you 'ld spare your spoons: you
shall have two noble partners with you; the old Duchess of
Norfolk, and Lady Marquess Dorset: will these please you?
Once more, my Lord of Winchester, I charge you,
Embrace and love this man.

    GAR.   With a true heart   170
And brother-love I do it.

    CRAN.   And let heaven
Witness how dear I hold this confirmation.

    KING. Good man, those joyful tears show thy true heart:
The common voice, I see, is verified
Of thee, which says thus: 'Do my Lord of Canterbury
A shrewd turn, and he is your friend for ever.'
Come, lords, we trifle time away; I long
To have this young one made a Christian.
As I have made ye one, lords, one remain;
So I grow stronger, you more honour gain.   [*Exeunt.* 180

SCENE IV. *The Palace Yard.*

Noise and tumult within. Enter Porter *and his* Man.

    PORT. You 'll leave your noise anon, ye rascals: do you take
the court for Paris-garden? ye rude slaves, leave your gaping.

    [*Within*] 'Good master porter, I belong to the larder.'

    PORT. Belong to the gallows, and be hanged, ye rogue!
Is this a place to roar in? Fetch me a dozen crab-tree staves, and
strong ones: these are but switches to 'em. I 'll scratch your heads:
you must be seeing christenings? do you look for ale and cakes
here, you rude rascals?

MAN. Pray, sir, be patient: 'tis as much impossible—
Unless we sweep 'em from the door with cannons—   10
To scatter 'em, as 'tis to make 'em sleep
On May-day morning; which will never be:
We may as well push against Powle's as stir 'em.

PORT. How got they in, and be hang'd?

MAN. Alas, I know not; how gets the tide in?
As much as one sound cudgel of four foot—
You see the poor remainder—could distribute,
I made no spare, sir.

PORT.   You did nothing, sir.

MAN. I am not Samson, nor Sir Guy, nor Colbrand,
To mow 'em down before me: but if I spared any   20
That had a head to hit, either young or old,
He or she, cuckold or cuckold-maker,
Let me ne'er hope to see a chine again;
And that I would not for a cow, God save her!

[*Within*] 'Do you hear, master porter?'

PORT. I shall be with you presently, good master puppy. Keep
the door close, sirrah.

MAN. What would you have me do?

PORT. What should you do, but knock 'em down by the
dozens? Is this Moorfields to muster in? or have we some strange   30
Indian with the great tool come to court, the women so besiege
us? Bless me, what a fry of fornication is at door! On my Christian
conscience, this one christening will beget a thousand; here will
be father, godfather, and all together.

MAN. The spoons will be the bigger, sir. There is a fellow
somewhat near the door, he should be a brazier by his face, for,
o' my conscience, twenty of the dog-days now reign in 's nose;
all that stand about him are under the line, they need no other
penance: that fire-drake did I hit three times on the head, and
three times was his nose discharged against me; he stands there,   40
like a mortar-piece, to blow us. There was a haberdasher's wife
of small wit near him, that railed upon me till her pinked por-
ringer fell off her head, for kindling such a combustion in the
state. I missed the meteor once, and hit that woman, who cried
out 'Clubs!' when I might see from far some forty truncheon-
ers draw to her succour, which were the hope o' the Strand,
where she was quartered. They fell on; I made good my place:

at length they came to the broomstaff to me; I defied 'em still:
when suddenly a file of boys behind 'em, loose shot, delivered
such a shower of pebbles, that I was fain to draw mine honour 50
in and let 'em win the work: the devil was amongst 'em, I think,
surely.

    Port. These are the youths that thunder at a playhouse and
fight for bitten apples; that no audience, but the tribulation of
Tower-hill, or the limbs of Limehouse, their dear brothers, are
able to endure. I have some of 'em in Limbo Patrum, and there
they are like to dance these three days; besides the running banquet of two beadles that is to come.

Enter Lord Chamberlain.

Cham. Mercy o' me, what a multitude are here!
They grow still too; from all parts they are coming,   60
As if we kept a fair here. Where are these porters,
These lazy knaves? Ye have made a fine hand, fellows!
There's a trim rabble let in: are all these
Your faithful friends o' the suburbs? We shall have
Great store of room, no doubt, left for the ladies,
When they pass back from the christening.
    Port.   An 't please your honour,
We are but men; and what so many may do,
Not being torn a-pieces, we have done:
An army cannot rule 'em.
    Cham.   As I live,
If the king blame me for 't, I 'll lay ye all   70
By the heels, and suddenly; and on your heads
Clap round fines for neglect: ye 're lazy knaves;
And here ye lie baiting of bombards when
Ye should do service. Hark! the trumpets sound;
They 're come already from the christening:
Go, break among the press, and find a way out
To let the troop pass fairly, or I 'll find
A Marshalsea shall hold ye play these two months.
    Port. Make way there for the princess.
    Man.   You great fellow,
Stand close up, or I 'll make your head ache.   80
    Port. You i' the camlet, get up o' the rail;

I 'll peck you o'er the pales else.   [*Exeunt.*

SCENE V. *The Palace.*

Enter Trumpets, *sounding; then two* Aldermen, Lord Mayor, Garter,
   CRANMER, DUKE OF NORFOLK *with his marshal's staff,* DUKE
   OF SUFFOLK, *two* Noblemen *bearing great standing-bowls for the
   christening gifts; then four* Noblemen *bearing a canopy, under
   which the* DUCHESS OF NORFOLK, *godmother, bearing the child
   richly habited in a mantle, &c., train borne by a* Lady; *then follows
   the* MARCHIONESS DORSET, *the other godmother, and* Ladies. *The
   troop pass once about the stage, and* Garter *speaks.*

   GART. Heaven, from thy endless goodness, send prosperous
life, long, and ever happy, to the high and mighty princess of
England, Elizabeth!

Flourish. Enter KING *and Guard.*

   CRAN. [*Kneeling*] And to your royal grace, and the good queen,
My noble partners and myself thus pray:
All comfort, joy, in this most gracious lady,
Heaven ever laid up to make parents happy,
May hourly fall upon ye!
   KING.   Thank you, good lord archbishop:
What is her name?
   CRAN.   Elizabeth.
   KING.   Stand up, lord.
                                    [*The King kisses the child.*
With this kiss take my blessing: God protect thee!   10
Into whose hand I give thy life.
   CRAN.   Amen.
   KING. My noble gossips, ye have been too prodigal:
I thank ye heartily; so shall this lady,
When she has so much English.
   CRAN.   Let me speak, sir,
For heaven now bids me; and the words I utter
Let none think flattery, for they 'll find 'em truth.
This royal infant—heaven still move about her!—

Though in her cradle, yet now promises
Upon this land a thousand thousand blessings,
Which time shall bring to ripeness: she shall be—   20
But few now living can behold that goodness—
A pattern to all princes living with her,
And all that shall succeed: Saba was never
More covetous of wisdom and fair virtue
Than this pure soul shall be: all princely graces,
That mould up such a mighty piece as this is,
With all the virtues that attend the good,
Shall still be doubled on her: truth shall nurse her,
Holy and heavenly thoughts still counsel her:
She shall be loved and fear'd: her own shall bless her;   30
Her foes shake like a field of beaten corn,
And hang their heads with sorrow. Good grows with her:
In her days every man shall eat in safety,
Under his own vine, what he plants, and sing
The merry songs of peace to all his neighbours:
God shall be truly known; and those about her
From her shall read the perfect ways of honour,
And by those claim their greatness, not by blood.
Nor shall this peace sleep with her; but, as when
The bird of wonder dies, the maiden phoenix,   40
Her ashes new create another heir
As great in admiration as herself,
So shall she leave her blessedness to one—
When heaven shall call her from this cloud of darkness—
Who from the sacred ashes of her honour
Shall star-like rise, as great in fame as she was,
And so stand fix'd. Peace, plenty, love, truth, terror,
That were the servants to this chosen infant,
Shall then be his, and like a vine grow to him:
Wherever the bright sun of heaven shall shine,   50
His honour and the greatness of his name
Shall be, and make new nations: he shall flourish,
And, like a mountain cedar, reach his branches
To all the plains about him. Our children's children
Shall see this, and bless heaven.
    KING.   '   Thou speakest wonders.
    CRAN. She shall be, to the happiness of England,
An aged princess; many days shall see her,

And yet no day without a deed to crown it.
Would I had known no more! but she must die;
She must; the saints must have her; yet a virgin, 60
A most unspotted lily shall she pass
To the ground, and all the world shall mourn her.
  KING. O lord archbishop,
Thou hast made me now a man! never, before
This happy child, did I get any thing.
This oracle of comfort has so pleased me,
That when I am in heaven I shall desire
To see what this child does, and praise my Maker.
I thank ye all. To you, my good lord mayor,
And your good brethren, I am much beholding; 70
I have received much honour by your presence,
And ye shall find me thankful. Lead the way, lords:
Ye must all see the queen, and she must thank ye;
She will be sick else. This day, no man think
Has business at his house; for all shall stay:
This little one shall make it holiday.   [*Exeunt*.

THE EPILOGUE.

'Tis ten to one this play can never please
All that are here: some come to take their ease,
And sleep an act or two; but those, we fear,
We have frighted with our trumpets; so, 'tis clear,
They 'll say 'tis naught: others, to hear the city
Abused extremely, and to cry 'That's witty!'
Which we have not done neither; that, I fear,
All the expected good we 're like to hear
For this play at this time, is only in
The merciful construction of good women;   10
For such a one we show'd 'em: if they smile,
And say 'twill do, I know, within a while
All the best men are ours; for 'tis ill hap,
If they hold when their ladies bid 'em clap.